Dr. Thomas Zachariah

Applying Knowledge Management to Build-to-Order Processes in Manufacturing and Service Companies

Anchor Academic
Publishing

Zachariah, Thomas: Applying Knowledge Management to Build-to-Order Processes in Manufacturing and Service Companies, Hamburg, Anchor Academic Publishing 2017

Buch-ISBN: 978-3-96067-116-9
PDF-eBook-ISBN: 978-3-96067-616-4
Druck/Herstellung: Anchor Academic Publishing, Hamburg, 2017

Bibliografische Information der Deutschen Nationalbibliothek:
Die Deutsche Nationalbibliothek verzeichnet diese Publikation in der Deutschen
Nationalbibliografie; detaillierte bibliografische Daten sind im Internet über
http://dnb.d-nb.de abrufbar.

Bibliographical Information of the German National Library:
The German National Library lists this publication in the German National Bibliography.
Detailed bibliographic data can be found at: http://dnb.d-nb.de

© Anchor Academic Publishing, Imprint der Diplomica Verlag GmbH
Hermannstal 119k, 22119 Hamburg
http://www.diplomica-verlag.de, Hamburg 2017
Printed in Germany

Abstract

Knowledge management differs from expert systems as the latter are more attuned to integrating all available sources of data, information, and knowledge into a single, unified system of record. Capturing tacit and explicit knowledge and its use in streamlining business processes is also what differentiates knowledge management systems from expert systems. The purpose of this study is to define practical, pragmatic, and replicable approaches to knowledge management as it relates to the build-to-order and mass-customization strategies of manufacturing and services companies in the United States. The overall research question guiding this study is: How is knowledge management being used today to streamline and make more efficient the service strategies of manufacturing and services companies? The research is descriptive and empirical in nature because the primary data were collected using the survey method, through fact-finding techniques such as a questionnaire. The results show the integration of increasing role-based knowledge management in the workflow of a company. Knowledge management accelerates the exchange of aligned cost reduction to IT strategies for the use of knowledge to create a greater financial value. In this study, it was found that the degree of maturity of the company in the transition from cost-reduction strategies on the use of knowledge fails with respect to competitive strength. From this study, a knowledge-sharing maturity model is derived, which illustrates how the level and extent of knowledge exploitation in build-to-order and quote-to-order strategies have a long-term impact on financial performance. From these findings on how a company manages its knowledge in its build-to-order and quote-to-order strategy, a causal relationship emerges, which aligns well with a multi-stage maturity model. One of the main objectives of the study is to determine how the customer churn rate can be reduced. By optimizing business processes, companies can increase customer satisfaction while reducing the Days Sales Outstanding levels over time. A better alignment of processes with customer requirements would help to achieve higher margins.

Keywords: Knowledge Management, Build-to-Order, Quote-to-Order

Table of Contents

List of Figures

List of Tables

List of Abbreviations

BPM	-	Business Process Management
CFO	-	Chief Financial
CIO	-	Chief Information Officer
CMO	-	Chief Marketing Officer
CRM	-	Customer Relationship Management
DDSN	-	Demand Driven Supply Network
DMAIC	-	Define, Measure, Analyze, Improve and Control
DOM	-	Distributed Order Management
DSO	-	Days Sales Outstanding
EDI	-	Electronic Data Interchange
ERP	-	Enterprise Resource Planning
FG	-	Finished Goods
KPI	-	Key Performance Indicators
MDM	-	Master Data Management
NPDI	-	New Product Development and Introduction
POI	-	Perfect Order Index
ROI	-	Return on Investment
ROIC	-	Return on Invested Capital
SaaS	-	Software-as-a-Service
SOA	-	Service Oriented Architecture
TQM	-	Total Quality Management
VoC	-	Voice of the Customer
WIP	-	Work in Process

Chapter 1: Overview

Supply chain management in a global world is challenged by new technologies. Therefore, the high speed with which changes take place at the Distributed Order Management (DOM) and Enterprise Resource Planning (ERP) forces many companies to assume sales strategies for contract manufacturing and mass customization. In the sales strategy for contract manufacturing, there are different variants of assemble-to-order: from those where only a small percentage of the product is customized individually, to engineer-to-order, where most of the features of a product are based on customer specifications. Study results indicate that with greater accuracy and speed of data integration, and collaborative agreement in the supply chain, the accuracy of execution increases (Novack & Thomas, 2004). Performance criteria in this area of supply chain management and DOMs are the Perfect-Order criteria (Hofman, 2004).

This research study is to determine how companies integrate knowledge management systems in build-to-order processes to achieve a flawless execution. The benefits of knowledge-management systems and their alignment with customer requirements and classification schemes have an accelerating effect on the accuracy and agility of build-to-order systems. Measuring the integration of knowledge-management systems and build-to-order processes using the Perfect-Order criteria give insights into how the profitability of strategies of product customization can be enhanced by streamlined operations of product definition, quoting, pricing, and order execution.

Background Study

Through disseminating products and services on the principle of mass customization, companies urgently need to integrate their extensive knowledge-management systems into the pricing, product configuration, quotation, and support activities underlying their sales activities. All these platforms and systems for knowledge management for pricing, quoting, product configuration, and deployment of services supply the catalyst for transactions and product availability. The supply chain has been found to be the principal source of knowledge that must penetrate the corporate structure, and ensure synchronization of companies and general market requirements (Dyer & Nobeoka, 2000). To ensure the viability of build-to-order, configure-to-order, and engineer-to-order strategies, a high degree of process and information integration in knowledge-management systems across the supply chain is necessary. The better these supply systems are integrated into the build-to-order systems, online product configurators, pricing systems, and service systems, the higher the probability that all individual contracts can be executed and delivered flawlessly. According to the Perfect-Order concept, close integration of the different supply systems, sales systems, and platforms such as web-based build-to-order, configure-to-order, and engineer-to-order, along with configurable and knowledge-management systems at an appropriate synchronization, comply with or even undercut predetermined customer delivery dates. The Perfect-Order criteria were originally designed to measure supply chain performance (Hofman, 2004). In integrating the operational capacity, the efficiency of cash-to-cash process flows, and a company's ability to forecast demand accuracy, the Perfect-Order criteria are a reliable performance indicator in traditional environments.

Over time, the Perfect-Order criteria enable the online sales strategies of mass customization, contract manufacturing (build-to-order or configure-to-order) and construction-oriented production (engineer-to-order) to be incorporated into the business processes of manufacturers. The company Dell was largely responsible for the successful concept of online sales of build-to-order PCs. In fact, the annual revenue of several billion which Dell recorded after the system reached a global scale led many companies to pursue extending their strategies of mass customization and contract manufacturing (Fields, 2006).

Many high-tech companies are interested in establishing performance criteria based on Perfect-Order-based strategies that are designed to implement their build-to-order, configure-to-order, and engineer-to-order strategies as efficiently, and make the companies as profitable, as possible (Fields, 2006). The Perfect-Order criteria were initially applied to the items with the highest inventory turnover, which was a high commodification, as inventory turnover was crucial for profitability. In these early platforms, knowledge-management integration aimed to facilitate data integration for products and product combinations. Dell performed the integration of knowledge-management systems in product configurations only gradually, because each system uses a different data format, different product definitions, and completely different ERP systems (Fields, 2006). Therefore, Dell often introduces new products only after considerable delays in the market, and the online systems for catalog and order management often have to be completely redefined, to compensate for the lack of knowledge-management support for the supply systems of the enterprise (Fields, 2006). Many other companies have since experienced similar problems in introducing new products which, in some industries such as the high-tech sector, make up to 60% of total revenue in a new product line. In the initial launch of its online strategy, Dell found that a lack of integration of knowledge-management systems, and the inefficiency of the build-to-order, configure-to-order, and engineer-to-order strategies, meant the online sales strategies were severely impaired. After Dell had learned the importance of knowledge-management systems and supply-chain data from the business model, the company chose a new approach to managing its strategies of product adaptation (Fields, 2006). Dell applied the Perfect-Order criteria to their specific business needs and developed a series of balanced scorecards and performance criteria to evaluate how effectively the company integrated its knowledge-management systems and supply-chain performance, and the accuracy of executing its strategy of mass customization.

The Perfect Order Index (POI) effectively contributed to promoting customer satisfaction and gave the company a base for evaluating their performance in terms of customer satisfaction (Columbus, 2008). The POI results showed increased customer loyalty to the company via repeat purchases, and a relationship between increasing Perfect-Order performance and long-term increase customer profitability was recognized (Columbus, 2008). This relationship of Perfect-Order performance with long-term customer loyalty and profitability can be seen in the areas of complex manufacturing, high technology, special vehicles, and medical products and services (Columbus, 2008).

The index shows the effectiveness of the use of knowledge-management systems for highly complex engineer-to-order products with high profit margins, and cost-effective standard products sold only based on price and availability. The use of Perfect-Order criteria to measure the overall performance of a Demand Driven Supply Network (DDSN) is also of great benefit, because a common industry-wide base is provided, and the cross-industry integration of these systems can be evaluated (Barrett, 2007). The implementation speed of a mass customization strategy is directly affected by the extent to which the knowledge-management systems, from catalog management to expert systems, are integrated into guided selling and complex engineer-to-order processes (Columbus, 2008). This study is to determine how knowledge-management systems can lead, with supply-chain data, to a more accurate long-term coordination of build-to-order, configure-to-order, and engineer-to-order sales strategies via the channels selected by a company. The possibility of predicting customer satisfaction and loyalty based on the respective level of the POI will ultimately revolutionize these three order systems integration and real-time systems and platforms development (Columbus, 2008).

Research Design

To determine the impact of integrating knowledge-management systems and build-to-order applications with Perfect-Order performance, the coordination and collaboration of leading members from the community of high-tech manufacturing is required. Therefore, contact with the American Electronics Association and other professional organizations that measure key financial metrics was considered. As this study was exclusively conducted online, contacting the employees of these bodies and members of these associations regarding participation in this research program was crucial for its success.

The participants in this research were the Chief Financial Officers or heads of finance departments of manufacturing and service industries, as they know the process and frameworks introduced to apply knowledge to build-to-order, configure-to-order, and engineer-to-order strategies and feature data to calculate the POI for their businesses.

The web survey tool Zoomerang was used to create the survey and was sent via email as a link. The survey includes a questionnaire that relates to several comparative studies on knowledge-management integration and product-configuration systems (build-to-order components), and the current and future use of performance indicators for the supply chain. As far as possible within the framework of online survey tools, the survey also worked with graphics to ensure ease of use and a better understanding. Respondents also indicated how they used scarce resources for introducing a new product, or the importance of knowledge-management systems for making price adjustments during the life-cycle of a product. In addition, the POI was included in the questionnaire to find out whether the companies surveyed established a relationship between Perfect-Order performance and customer satisfaction.

Research Questions

The purpose of this study is to understand the application of knowledge management to optimize the build-to-order process in manufacturing and service companies. The overall research question guiding this study is: How is knowledge management being used today to streamline and make more efficient service strategies of manufacturing and services companies?

These questions critically analyze the metrics used by companies to verify their knowledge-management systems' performance. They also assess how effective knowledge-management systems are for preventing incorrect orders and increasing customer satisfaction. These questions are relevant to the overall research objectives, and help assess the processes that are used in applying knowledge management.

Summary

The dynamics by which the performance of build-to-order products is influenced by knowledge-management systems, and is carried out via Perfect-Order criteria related to the collaborative agreement in the supply chain, are an important predictor of customer satisfaction. The causal relationship between these interactive systems and long-term customer loyalty and significant satisfaction for all enterprises operating in business sectors with rapid inventory turnover is crucial, especially for goods such as high-tech products.

Chapter 2: Literature Review

Creating more opportunities for revenue growth with build-to-order, configure-to-order, and engineer-to-order strategies are predicated on a well-defined and highly-integrated series of strategies that unify selling efforts and supply chains. The intention of this literature review is to evaluate how the standard metrics of performance included in the hierarchy of supply chain metrics are accelerated through the efficient use of knowledge-management systems and strategies.

This chapter addresses the research objective of evaluating the contributory effects of knowledge management to mass customization and build-to-order strategies within a manufacturing company. It also addresses the second research objective, namely, to determine the causality in knowledge-management system integration with build-to-order and mass-customization system performance when varying integration technologies are used, these ranging from Electronic Data Interchange (EDI) to RosettaNet and real-time XML integration. It is important to note that, regardless of how integrated or all-encompassing a given standard is for data interchange, the one common denominator agreed on by most businesses is how to manage transactions. This is a key takeaway from this literature review. This chapter also discusses the third research objective, that is, to define a series of dashboard metrics that can be used for evaluating the level of knowledge-management system contribution to custom configuration and quoting accuracy across all channels a manufacturer sells through. Using the Hierarchy of Supply Chain metrics shown in Figure 2 (Hofman, 2004), a maturity model for integrating knowledge-management systems with product-configuration platforms that enable the build-to-order and mass customization process is also defined and presented (AMR Research Report, 2005). Finally, this chapter also analyzes a framework for quantifying the performance gains of integrating knowledge-management systems and product-configuration strategies.

15

The ability of companies to orchestrate the many disparate, legacy, and, often, stand-alone systems that are required to optimize the build-to-order selling and production processes is predicated on how effectively the core concepts, frameworks, and strategies contribute to the efficient and profitable performance of build-to-order selling and production strategies on a global scale. These concepts and frameworks can serve to galvanize a strategy in the most effective and profitable direction, and provide a series of relevant metrics and key performance indicators (KPIs).

A critical catalyst in the theory of operations relating to build-to-order selling and production strategies is the reliance on Six Sigma methodologies that take variation out of core processes. The DMAIC (Define, Measure, Analyze, Improve, and Control) Model is extensively used throughout build-to-order selling and production strategies, to ensure consistency of processes and profitability by mitigating the costs of previously unpredictable processes. With these metrics, a heavy reliance on the supply-chain hierarchy of metrics is evident from the literature review, and also the need to quantify build-to-order strategies' performance over time. Six Sigma and DMAIC models are used to validate the scalability and reliability of a process, and the KPIs from the supply-chain hierarchy of metrics provide quantified evidence of performance gains. One of the most critical metrics is also Perfect Order, which is also discussed throughout this chapter. Taken together, all these metrics serve as a unifying, galvanizing catalyst that brings together all aspects of the build-to-order production workflows over time.

In evaluating the role of metrics and KPIs throughout the build-to-order process, it is also important to concentrate on the lag-time of these factors in quantifying overall strategy performance. It is common for the most financially-based metrics and KPIs to take up to nine months or a year to become evident from performance analysis (Columbus, 2008). On the other hand, the metrics and KPIs that are supply-chain centric and focused on transactions are typically visible within six months or less of initial strategy implementation (Hofman, 2004). Therefore, the literature review in this chapter defines a theory of operation that seeks to explain the lag-time in these financial versus operational measures of performance, and explains how companies' performance across industries varies drastically, depending on how they approach this concept of build-to-order selling and production strategies.

Defining Core Concepts and Frameworks for Build-to-Order Strategies

The most fundamental elements of build-to-order selling and production strategies are the series of strategic goals and objectives on which they are based, followed by the balanced scorecards and approaches to measuring, monitoring, and modifying strategy performance based on the findings. Taken together, the series of metrics must all contribute to a strategic view of the entire process and its contribution to the enterprise's profitability to be effective (AMR Research Report, 2003). Inherent in the best practices of build-to-order selling and production strategies is the design of analysis, evaluation, and continual improvement of each area of the process workflow to ensure continual improvement. The reliance on Six Sigma techniques for continually measuring, monitoring, and modifying the build-to-order selling and production strategies illustrate how pervasive the use of quality management and continuous improvement methodologies is in this area (Davison & Al-Shaghana, 2007).

The DMAIC Model is specifically relied on as a methodology to capture the process performance of build-to-order, assemble-to-order, configure-to-order, and engineer-to-order strategies and workflows. Six Sigma has been heavily relied on, because of the innate functionality and flexibility of the DMAIC Model for quickly determining the inter-process performance from the customers' standpoint, while considering the constraints under which a business operates (Raisinghani, Ette, Pierce, Cannon, & Daripaly, 2005). The Six Sigma DMAIC framework illustrates the framework as it relates to a lifecycle-based approach in managing customer-centric projects and programs, as shown in Figure 1 (Raisinghani et al., 2005).

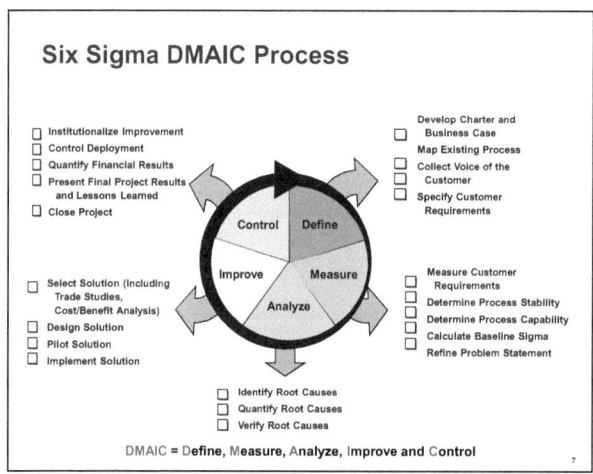

Figure 1. Six Sigma DMAIC Framework.

The Six Sigma DMAIC framework is extensively used as one of the core functional areas of measuring build-to-order performance, given its integration with Voice of the Customer (VoC) elements. While Six Sigma is often used as a means to measure just process-centric performance, it can also be used for evaluating the customer-oriented application responsiveness and accuracy (Davison & Al-Shaghana, 2007). The best DMAIC-based implementations throughout the build-

18

to-order strategies are heavily reliant on a continual update from customers on how well their experiences relate to their expectations, with Six Sigma measuring the difference between these two values (AMR Research Report, 2003). The ability of Six Sigma to be used for evaluating how effectively a quote-to-order strategy aligns with customer expectations is evident in how DMAIC-based results are often used to define which supply-chain metrics are used to evaluate overall business performance. The DMAIC Model is a means to define which metric in the hierarchy of supply-chain metrics is best to quantify the customer satisfaction, quoting the entire build-to-order strategy and its profitability (Davison & Al-Shaghana, 2007).

Studies also suggest the correlation between customer satisfaction and the profitability of companies which continually improve their build-to-order selling and production processes are especially strong in B2B markets (Raisinghani et al., 2005). This is because combining the DMAIC framework, its metrics of performance as they relate to process performance and continual improvement, and integrating supply chain metrics focuses a company's efforts towards creating an exceptional customer experience. Combining the DMAIC framework factors, use of selected metrics from the hierarchy of supply chain metrics, and the use of the VoC components of Six Sigma can transform a build-to-order strategy from being static and outdated to one which exceeds customers' expectations. The triad effect of these factors can transform business models over the long term by continually exceeding customer expectations as well.

Later in the chapter, the financial implications of excelling at build-to-order selling and production strategy are discussed for financial results. However, it is important to consider that only by having a stable Six Sigma platform with DMAIC-based strategies, anchored in supply-chain metrics, with metrics that quantify customer satisfaction, can any build-to-order selling and production strategy continually improve and contribute profits over time. The quantifiable nature of the process workflows that comprise build-to-order have just as much an effect on customer satisfaction as they do on the financial performance of firms; this point will also be reviewed in this chapter.

Theorists have argued the lag-time in the financial metrics of quote-to-order strategies is primarily attributed to customer expectations being slow in translating into customer lifetime value over time, often nine months or even a year into the standardization on a build-to-order strategy (Barrett, 2007). Six Sigma and the DMAIC Model are the foundation for evaluating process performance and its impact on operations, and when these approaches in evaluating performance are augmented with the hierarchy of supply-chain metrics, they become orders of magnitude more effective in streamlining the quote-to-order process over time (Raisinghani et al., 2005). Each of the attributes, KPIs, and metrics shown in Figure 2 (Hofman, 2004) add another element of insight into the DMAIC-based methodologies on which enterprises rely to streamline their quote-to-order strategies and supporting processes. This is a critical step in applying knowledge management to optimize the build-to-order process, as it brings insight, intelligence, and guidance into the planning, execution, monitoring, and measurement processes surrounding this complex selling and production strategy. Another aspect of selectively integrating metrics and KPIs from Figure 2 (Hofman, 2004) to increase the effectiveness of knowledge management in the build-to-order process is based on the inherent strengths and weaknesses of a given business model. Many of the metrics and KPIs provided in Figure 2 (Hofman, 2004) are applicable only to manufacturing-centric businesses. Creating an effective approach in defining which of the metrics in the hierarchy of supply-chain metrics are the most relevant to a given business model takes insight, and forward planning over time.

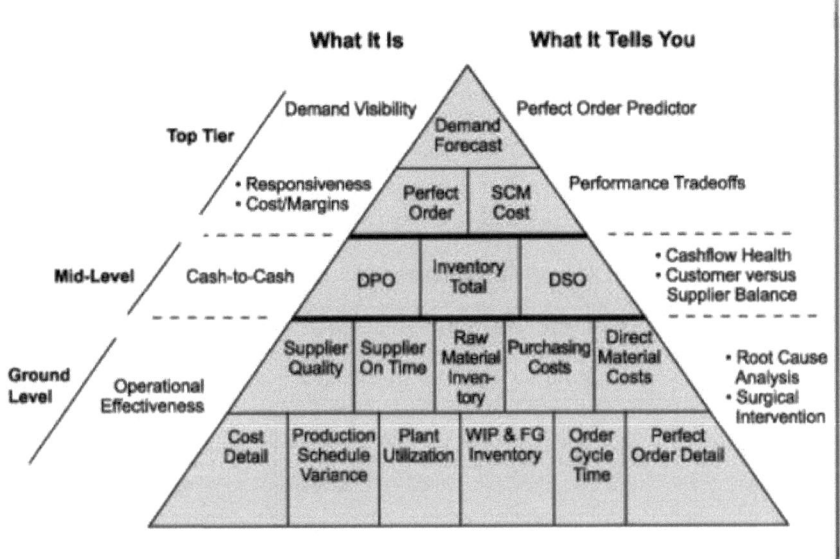

Figure 2. The Hierarchy of Supply-Chain Metrics.

Often, companies will go through a series of iterations to define which of the supply-chain metrics best fit their business model, given their unique needs and requirements (Hofman, 2004). Dell has done this several times, continually re-evaluating the supply-chain metrics and their relative importance in the broader corporate goals and objectives for their product configuration and build-to-order process workflows and programs (Fields, 2006). This continual re-evaluation of the metrics, KPIs, and methodologies that integrate them into lean manufacturing and Six Sigma strategies is critical for any enterprise to evolve over time (AMR Research Report, 2003). There is no "one and done" approach to managing change as it relates to these metrics for build-to-order selling workflows; rather, it is the continual re-evaluation of these metrics for their contribution to enterprise strategies, given the current overarching mission and vision of an organization (Barrett, 2007).

21

The ability to stay agile and market-focused, demand-driven, and continually focused on streamlining the supply chain through production and fulfillment, all driven by customer expectation, will revolutionize a company in the long run. Build-to-order strategies contribute to companies becoming more demand-driven. This has become so pervasive in highly-specialized manufacturing environments that the concept of a DDSN has begun to dominate the Sales & Operations Planning strategies of companies on a global scale (Barrett, 2007). The net effect of a well-managed product-configuration strategy is that of making an entire manufacturing and service strategy more market-driven and, therefore, more agile and capable of responding more effectively to market demands. While the costs of implementing a successfully functioning build-to-order strategy can be recaptured quickly, based on time and cost savings from having a more streamlined process, the focus on attaining Perfect Order is what many companies concentrate on as a key metric (Columbus, 2008). A Perfect Order occurs when all aspects are perfectly fulfilled, from the initial sourcing of products, the coordination of the production cycle in ERP systems, to the delivery of the finished product in perfect working conditions (Novack &Thomas, 2004).

The Perfect Order has grown in prominence because it measures how effective a company is in orchestrating its supply chain to selling strategies, interlinking production and logistics performance in the process (Columbus, 2008; Novack & Thomas, 2004). It has also emerged as the foundation for measuring how effectively a quote-to-order strategy is in translating process improvements into long-term knowledge generation and financial performance (Dyer & Nobeoka, 2000). The Financial Analysis of Knowledge Management Contribution to Product-Configuration Strategies, shown in Figure 3 (AMR Research Report, 2005), serves as a foundation to illustrate the effects of an effective build-to-order strategy on the long-term financial performance of a company. These contributions emanate from the ability to both streamline business processes to reduce costs, and make companies more effective at selling and long-term customer acquisition.

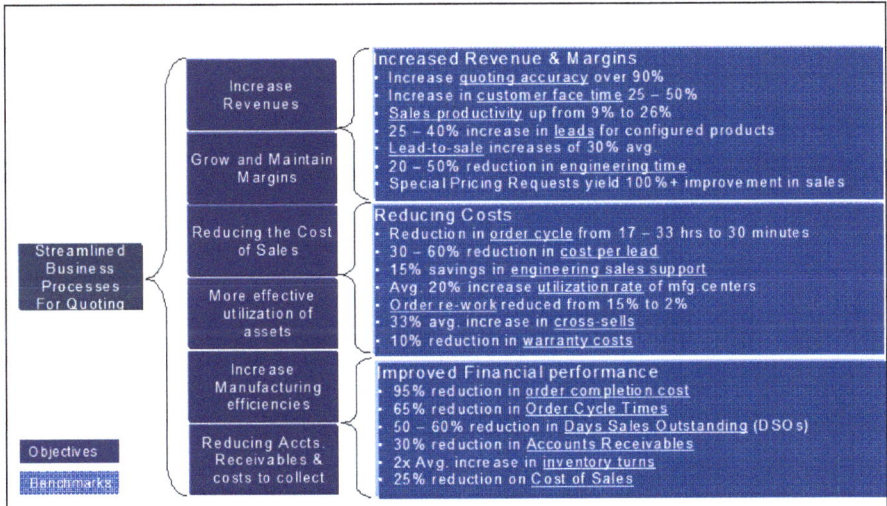

Figure 3. Financial Analysis of Knowledge Management Contribution to Product Configuration Strategies.

Mass customization and the ability to create products and services that precisely align with the needs of a given business are progressing rapidly. As a result, all available knowledge and insight within a business needs to be applied to the quote-to-order and build-to-order processes throughout organizations for the selling strategies to be profitable. Integrating the hierarchy of supply chain metrics into the Six Sigma and DMAIC frameworks provides companies with the ability to quickly interpret and respond to the unique requirements of their markets, while also staying centered on their core competencies. The result is the ability to innovate and continually grow new lines of business while staying centered on a core set of strengths. This ability to transition away from just make-to-stock products and embrace the innate variability of products built to customer demands is also critical for the continual evolution of companies. Entire industries are shifting their focus from the "one size fits all" mentality of production and choosing instead to concentrate on how to create unique and highly-differentiated products that align with customers' needs. This chapter defines how these components must interact with one another, supporting each other over time to ensure the smooth functioning of the build-to-order process workflows. Integrating Six Sigma, DMAIC, and the supply-chain hierarchy of performance metrics, companies can capitalize on their innate intelligence to modify their approaches to production, to make them more centered on the customer and their unique demands, and less on staying in a rigidly-defined structure that robs them of additional margin.

The Perfect Order Meets Knowledge Management

The era of intelligent manufacturing has arrived, brought about through integrating knowledge-management and mass-customization strategies, all unified as part of lean manufacturing and services strategies (Yeh, Liu, Shia, Cheng, & Huwang, 2008). Developing knowledge-management platforms capable of creating significant value by bringing tacit and explicit knowledge into the mass-customization process is also redefining discrete manufacturing today (Choudhary, Harding, & Tiwari, 2009). With the advent of intelligent manufacturing, analytics and metrics of performance, including KPIs, play a central role in aligning supply chains and manufacturing capabilities to customer demand.

The Era of Intelligent Manufacturing and Six Sigma

Intelligent manufacturing is also leading to simplifying complex sell-side and customer-facing processes, by using Six Sigma performance analysis and improvement methodologies (Davison & Al-Shaghana, 2007). Attaining high consistency on the core process areas, including quoting, pricing, product configuration, build-to-order, configure-to-order, and engineer-to-order,

24

is essential for this business strategy to flourish. Six Sigma is a quality-management technique that seeks to reduce the variation and unpredictability in each process by using the DMAIC Model, as shown in Figure 1 (Raisinghani et al., 2005).

The Six Sigma DMAIC framework is heavily reliant on continual feedback from customers as to how well-aligned a given process is to their needs, or not. At the center of the DMAIC Model is a process area called VoC which seeks to quantify the impact of the process change on customers' lifetime value, and their relative satisfaction with a purchasing or service process (Raisinghani et al., 2005). The Six Sigma DMAIC Framework has been used extensively to streamline the quote-to-order, build-to-order, configure-to-order, and engineer-to-order workflows across many of the manufacturers who rely on these selling and manufacturing strategies (Raisinghani et al., 2005). Dell continues an aggressive quality-management program internally to continually gain greater insights into how to improve their quote-to-order, product-configuration, and system-configuration selling processes, and also the services processes scaled globally on their Intranet sites (Foreman, Gallien, Alspaugh, Lopez, Bhatnagar, Teo & Dubois, 2010). Dell is learning, like many other manufacturers across discrete and process manufacturing operations, the greater the knowledge integration in their continual efforts to improve these strategies, the greater the performance gains over time (Foreman et al., 2010). Knowledge has become an accelerator of process improvement, and the DMAIC Model has opened new avenues of improving build-to-order, configure-to-order, and engineer-to-order process accuracy, performance, and profitability over time. Of the many insights gained from the efforts, Dell is making to integrate knowledge management into these core selling and manufacturing strategies and processes, one of the most unforeseen by Dell's senior management is the impact unstructured content makes on the company's ability to deliver the Perfect Order (Foreman et al., 2010). Dell has found that many companies using the Six Sigma DMAIC framework to improve mass customization processes have data that need to complete the most critical tasks for orders is unstructured. The analysis also showed that approximately 80% of the data relied on for quality-management decision-making within Dell was unstructured (Foreman et al., 2010). Integrating knowledge management delivers measurable financial impacts quickly by capitalizing on unstructured content (Lahl, 2011).

The DMAIC Model is one of the several catalysts that unify knowledge management overall, and unstructured content or tacit knowledge specifically, with the mass customization strategies of companies. Studies indicate the greatest value of the DMAIC Model lies in being able to define new processes for quickly gaining access to, aggregating, and transforming unstructured data into scalable taxonomies and frameworks. The studies Dell undertook show how significant managing tacit knowledge can be to attaining high performance and profitability levels over the long term (Foreman et al., 2010). Dell is discovering the faster they can capture tacit knowledge and integrate it into the mass customization process, the greater the reduction in order errors and incorrect pricing, and the less frequent the requirement to completely rework orders over time, including in-field retrofitting of servers. Therefore, Dell has admitted to having a special team of quality-management professionals specifically assigned to managing the refurbishment and retrofit requirements of in-warranty high-end servers and systems in the field which were incorrectly configured because of incomplete product knowledge (Foreman et al., 2010). While Dell does not disclose these figures, it is clear the costs are well over $1M per year to replace incorrectly configured servers, workstations, and entire networks in the field. This is done quietly, as Dell does not want competitors to know, and wants to ensure that other enterprises, or very large accounts, do not find out which areas of the custom-quoting and build-to-order processes are weak because of tacit knowledge, including unstructured and structured content, not being completely integrated into the process areas. This concept of a SWAT team to solve major order inaccuracies in the field is also prevalent in the healthcare and medical products industry. One Chief Information Officer (CIO) discussed in group QAD stated the medical cabinets produced by his company can, in 50% of cases, deliver the wrong configuration to a hospital as tacit knowledge of the specific requirements has not been correctly captured. He stated the configurations sold by the sales teams are down and, at times, cannot even be built by the production center. The result is that in one month, nearly 50% of production had to be retrofitted in the field, because of a lack of knowledge-management integration to the build-to-order, configure-to-order, and engineer-to-order processes.

Knowledge-Management and Product-Configuration Strategies

From a quality-management standpoint, integrating knowledge management into product configuration is delivering insights into how to amend these processes to be more accurate, efficient, and customer-centric (Foreman et al., 2010). Dell and others did not initially see the benefits of integrating enterprise-wide knowledge management into their product-configuration strategies from a lifecycle perspective. What changed this was the decision on the part of manufacturers to begin mining product configuration data to determine how this unstructured content could revolutionize the new product development and introduction (NPDI) process (Sana, 2011). As this initial discovery of product knowledge being unstructured yet highly valuable in defining customers' unmet needs, companies including Dell, IBM, and other service industries today regularly capture and transform the product configuration data left from customers' online sessions into new sources of tacit knowledge (Hong, Xue, & Tu, 2010). Aggregating and transforming this data from product-configuration design sessions that potential prospects for products or services leave abandoned is being used to redefine product platforms, and create disruptive innovation to the product-configuration process which was not possible before (Song & Kusiak, 2009).

Tacit knowledge capture and its use in build-to-order, configure-to-order, and engineer-to-order processes, regardless of how it is captured, is also leading to a more direct connection between the breadth and depth of options offered, based on customer preferences, and higher product quality and sales achieved (Raisinghani et al., 2005). Only those product options, configurations, and workflows that show potential for delivering the highest incidence of success are included in the Bill of Materials and product-configuration workflows over time (Lahl, 2011). The knowledge gain, and organizing taxonomies to aggregate unstructured content, are providing guidance to many manufacturing and services companies, specifically, for example, regarding which aspects of a given product design or functionality area of a build-to-order product need to be brought forward in the product roadmap and product lifecycle of a given series of solutions (Davison & Al-Shaghana, 2007). This is being done using product constraint engines, which have the ability to define an optimization path through the many options available in a given series of product and pricing options. This is also an area of the build-to-order, configure-to-order, and engineer-to-order process workflows where knowledge management is moving beyond the areas of just the selling process, and also making major contributions to the product-development and design strategies of companies (Novack &Thomas, 2004). Using constraint-based technologies, companies are also achieving the highest possible profitability on a per-unit basis by using knowledge management and Six Sigma procedures and processes (Hong, Xue, & Tu, 2010).

It is becoming increasingly common for manufacturing companies which have been successful in transforming tacit knowledge into a product design, product development, and pricing, to focus on integrating the data into Six Sigma process-improvement strategies (Kenett, 2009). Combining Six Sigma insights gained and the use of constraint-based software technologies, including those based on decision-support software, companies are able to define what incremental changes in process areas will have a corresponding effect on profitability. The result is a significant impact on process-timing performance metrics, followed by significant savings from a profitability standpoint over time, typically within 12 months of a major shift in process performance occurring based on tacit knowledge integration (Song & Kusiak, 2009). Dell reports that Six Sigma is one of the several Total Quality Management (TQM) initiatives in use which were originally meant to better manage product quality and compliance, but which are today being used to streamline product configuration and mass customization strategies across all product strategies in the company (Foreman et al., 2010). Dell has also found, like several other manufacturers, that 80% of all content in their companies is unstructured, yet most crucial for streamlining production and optimizing service-related strategies using constraint-based modeling (Tseng, Leeper, Banda, Herren, Ford, 2003). An adjunct area of these constraint-based modeling efforts and strategies has been the use of unstructured data analysis to add further depth and insight into Customer Relationship Management (CRM) systems, including the Master Data Management (MDM) platforms that serve as the system of record (Raisinghani et al., 2005). One of the primary objectives of this research effort is to validate the causality of all forms of knowledge management having a significant effect on the build-to-order, configure-to-order, and engineer-to-order strategy performance of companies over time. Based on the accessing, aggregating, and transforming of tacit knowledge within manufacturers, it has been proven there are significant gains in mass-customization strategy performance (Foreman et al., 2010). It has also been proven from secondary research that mining and aggregating product-configuration data from abandoned product design, assemble-to-order, build-to-order, configure-to-order, and engineer-to-order sessions can have a significant effect on product-design effectiveness, and a resulting impact on profitability over the long term (Song & Kusiak, 2009).

The literature review so far makes the observation that a maturity model is evident in how effectively companies from services and manufacturing sectors are integrating knowledge management into their product-configuration, to-order and mass-customization strategies. The more pervasive the level of integration, the greater the level of profit potential by influencing the next generation of product strategies, pricing, and discontinuation of product options that may drive people away from a given product line (Song & Kusiak, 2009). The irony that this research effort also looks to explore is that, by offering so many options and alternatives in a product-configuration strategy that are not aligned to specific users' needs, prospects may be driven away from, not attracted towards, a given product configuration or service set (Song & Kusiak, 2009). This finding would have major implications on the resulting supply chains and their performance over time, including the production inventory levels across all stocking centers, distribution centers, and production tagging areas (Sana, 2011). This would also be the area of a maturity model where the most significant amounts of cash would be tied up, as inventory and material costs in many manufacturing companies are second only to the costs of payroll and raw materials for production. From these observations in the maturity model, it is also evident that adopting KPIs and metrics of performance differentiates those companies which are achieving the highest levels of knowledge-management integration in their product-configuration, to-order, and mass-customization strategies. The next section of the literature review addresses the objective of defining the KPIs and metrics for the study and sets the foundation for the initial hierarchy of metrics that will be used for defining the maturity model and balanced framework. Creating both the maturity model and the balanced framework will be based on the results of the methodology, once completed.

Defining KPIs and Metrics of Performance

The hierarchy of supply chain metrics continued to be relied on most, out of the many different KPIs and metrics of performance, to evaluate the use of knowledge management in product-configuration, to-order, and mass-customization strategies (Hofman, 2004). The Perfect Order, a measure of order accuracy, transaction velocity, and demand visibility throughout an organization's value chain, is included in this hierarchy of metrics. The hierarchy of metrics originally evolved from companies who had a strong reliance on pick-pack-ship operations throughout their supply chains, and whose inventory turns were the most critical factor in determining profitability (Novack & Thomas, 2004). The more frequent the inventory turns, the greater the financial performance, including maximizing Return on Invested Capital (ROIC), which has also been relied on as a measure of customer satisfaction and lifetime value over the long term (Columbus, 2008). The hierarchy of supply chain metrics provides an overview of how each of the specific metrics combines to predict Perfect-Order performance, as shown in Figure 2 (Hofman, 2004). The hierarchy builds on operational effectiveness, leading to the cash-to-cash cycle that includes quote-to-order and quote-to-cash process workflows. The hierarchy continues with an assessment of the top tier of metrics that define relative profitability, including Supply Chain Management tradeoffs and Perfect-Order performance, thereby providing an ecosystem of analytics to evaluate company performance (Hofman, 2004).

The Perfect Order metric and hierarchy of supply chain metrics have become engrained into the operations of manufacturers who rely on make-to-stock, build-to-order, configure-to-order, and engineer-to-order selling and manufacturing strategies over time. This was due in large part to the success that GE, HP, IBM, Cisco, Dell and others have had in using the series of metrics in the hierarchy to better manage the measurement of knowledge integration into the build-to-order, configure-to-order, and engineer-to-order strategies and systems of companies. Dell, in fact, has used these metrics to evaluate how effective integrating front-office to back-office systems is throughout their company, and how effectively tacit knowledge is being captured and used in each of the product-configuration workflows (Fields, 2006).

Using the Perfect Order metric as a measure of knowledge-management integration throughout a company has also proven effective at ingraining a culture of accountability and performance into organizational cultures. Integrating tacit and explicit knowledge into Six Sigma quality improvement of mass-customization strategies continues to be instrumental in completely redefining organizational cultures as well (Davison & Al-Shaghana, 2007). This shift in the organizational structures, cultures, and values of companies has been of particular interest to many high-technology companies, whose cultures are already highly-focused on metrics. Adding the Perfect Order metric is seen as giving the ability to bring even greater levels of accountability, transparency, and trust into the build-to-order, configure-to-order, and engineer-to-order strategies. This move, from a cultural standpoint, is also seen as a way to bring greater profitability to supply chains and fulfillment operations throughout an organization. Studies of manufacturers who have successfully made this transition show that once a culture has been infused with a very high level of accountability and performance overall, the level of financial performance also increases (Davison & Al-Shaghana, 2007). This also supports the contention that the maturity model of knowledge-management integration with the build-to-order, configure-to-order, and engineer-to-order workflows, systems, and strategies of companies does deliver greater levels of accuracy and, eventually, profits. This link between knowledge-management integration and to-order strategies is also validated from the ROIC being achieved in manufacturing-centric businesses that, over time, attain higher levels of production utilization (Zhen, Jiang, & Song, 2011). Manufacturers are relying on the Perfect Order metric as a means to evaluate just how much more transaction velocity they are achieving over time as a result of integrating tacit and explicit knowledge into their to-order strategies as well. The introduction of the POI is specifically meant to address this area of the hierarchy's contribution to measuring customer satisfaction, and its effect on profitability over the long term (Columbus, 2008). The reliance on the POI within companies is continuing to gain momentum and consistently seen as a measure of how well a build-to-order, configure-to-order, and engineer-to-order system is operating (Columbus, 2008). From the perspective of the operations teams within a business, the POI determines if the process-system integration has considered every possible variation in mass-customization workflows. It will also define how effectively knowledge-management systems are being used for the complex, high-margin, engineer-to-order products relative to the low-end, commoditized products that are sold on price and availability alone. Using the Perfect Order as a metric to measure the overall performance of a DDSN is also invaluable in that it provides a common basis for evaluating these systems being integrated within and across industries (Barrett, 2007). The velocity of a given mass-customization strategy is directly reflected by how well the knowledge-management systems, from catalog management through expert-level systems, are integrated into the online ordering, guided selling, and more complex engineering-to-order workflows (Columbus, 2008). The proposed research seeks to validate how knowledge-management systems, when combined with supply-chain intelligence, can lead to a more precise alignment of build-to-order, configure-to-order, and engineer-to-order selling strategies through whatever channels a company chooses to rely on over the long term. Being able to predict customer satisfaction and loyalty by the relative level of the POI will eventually revolutionize how these systems are integrated with one another, leading to real-time-based system platforms supporting them (Columbus, 2008).

Knowledge Management Contributions to Build-To-Order Strategies

The premise of this research is that the greater the knowledge management within a build-to-order, configure-to-order, and engineer-to-order strategy, the greater the process efficiency created and, over time, the greater the profitability. An example that puts this premise into pragmatic terms is presented in this section of the literature review. Looking at the workflows for a specific engine manufacturer who has agreed to participate in this analysis on condition of anonymity because of the sensitive nature of the data presented, it is evident that without knowledge management integrated into the to-order process, business would often be lost. On average, it takes this globally-known electric engine manufacturer about 25 days to get a quote completed, as shown in Figure 4 (AMR Research Report, 2005). Competitors have the ability to quote and deliver prototypes in 15 days on rushed schedules and have re-defined their work teams to create this level of performance by embedding knowledge management into each quoting and proposal application online, globally. This means their competitors can produce a quote in minutes from anywhere in the world the Internet is available, as the quoting, pricing, and product-configuration systems all have knowledge management integrated directly within the customer quoting and CRM systems. The company used in this example has electric engine producing plants in the U.S. and Europe. The lag-time for knowledge management in manual workflows shown in Figure 4 is further exacerbated by this lack of real-time knowledge-sharing (AMR Research Report, 2005). Tacit and explicit knowledge within the R&D centers throughout Europe had been bottlenecked and could not be transmitted quickly to sales cycles throughout the U.S. and Asia. The result of this 20 – 25 day lag time was that the company was losing sales quickly in the emerging markets of China, Russia, Brazil, and India, as competitors had been able to create

knowledge-management systems quickly that could scale across these regions using Web-based

technologies, including social networks. Competitors had begun to create knowledge-sharing

networks using private-label versions of Facebook, password-protected versions of Twitter, and

intensive reliance on online tools, including an online configurator. Figure 4 shows the workflow

of a typical quote timeframe for a custom turbine engine built to customers' specifications (AMR

Research Report, 2005).

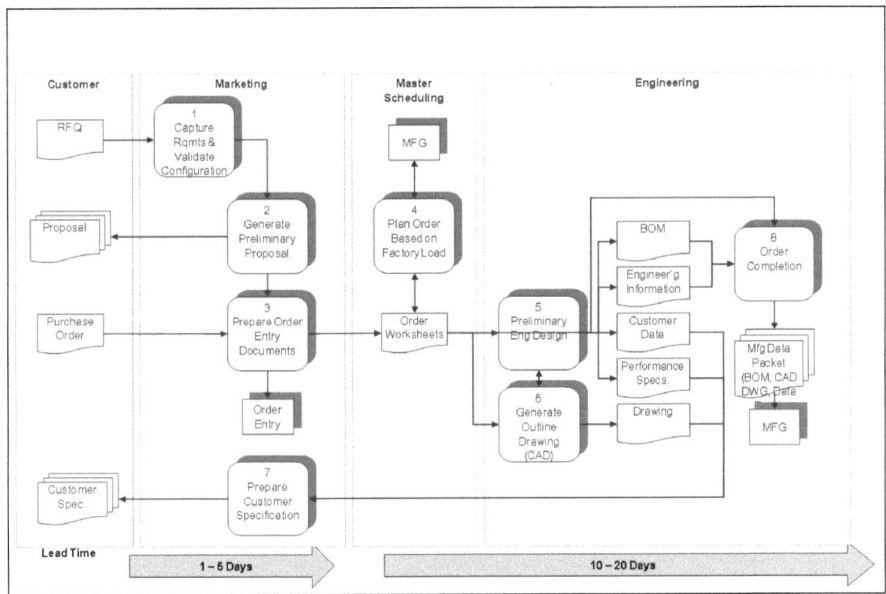

Figure 4. Manual Quote-to-Order Workflow Analysis.

When this electric engine manufacturer began gaining fewer deals than the number of quotes they

were producing, they realized that it was time to completely redefine the knowledge-management

strategy related to their quoting, pricing, and product configuration. The path they chose to pursue

to resolve this issue included the hierarchy of supply-chain metrics as a measure of process and role-based performance from a supply-chain standpoint (Hofman, 2004). The company also relied heavily on Business Process Management (BPM) techniques to find those process areas in need of the greatest modifications and improvements (Chang & Wang, 2011). The results of the re-engineering process and focus on streamlining the build-to-order process by integrating knowledge are shown in Figure 5 (AMR Research Report, 2005). This effort took approximately six months to complete and led to the quoting process being shortened to one hour. By capturing tacit and explicit knowledge effectively, and creating constraint rules for the data, the entire process had been simultaneously simplified and accelerated. In addition, tacit and explicit knowledge are now available 24/7 globally online.

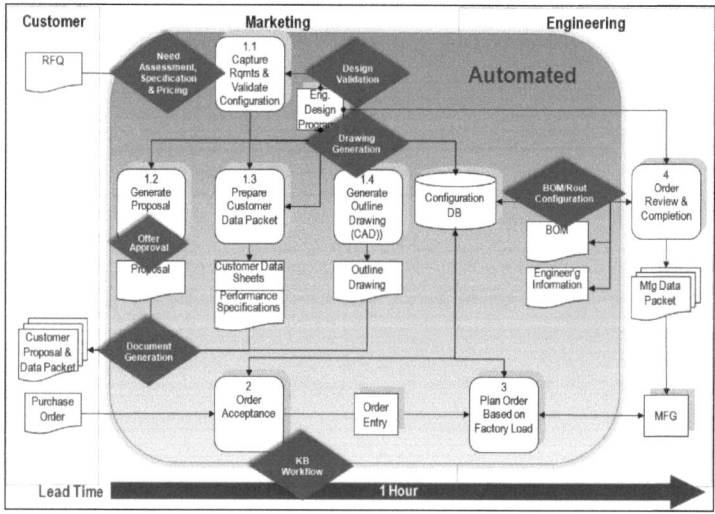

Figure 5. Streamlined Build-to-Order Process with Integrated Knowledge Management.

During the interview with the electrical engine manufacturer, their senior management advised that this accomplishment should not be looked at as a mechanistic achievement, but more

36

of a change management. The senior managers involved in this development said that getting the key R&D engineers to provide their tacit knowledge, and provide assistance for capturing explicit knowledge, made it possible to codify and then create taxonomies for the expertise involved. As is the case with many enterprise-wide projects, change management is the most crucial critical success factor there is in achieving significant financial gains from knowledge-management integration (Alstyne, Brynjolfsson, & Madnick, 1995).

Another insight gained from the analysis of the electric engine manufacturer and its gains in quoting performance and accuracy because of knowledge integration with the quoting process was the emergence of a knowledge-sharing network. Studies of the Toyota Production System, considered by many to be one of the most effective knowledge-sharing networks globally, show how knowledge-management strategies can translate expertise into the greatest competitive advantage of all (Dyer & Nobeoka, 2000). Harnessing knowledge inside an organization can drastically increase the ability of various departments, suppliers, stakeholders, and employees to achieve greater results over time. This is also the case with task and job ownership, two critical areas of development for change-management strategies to be effective over the long term (Alstyne, Brynjolfsson, & Madnick, 1995). The aggregate effect of these factors on Perfect Order metrics, as measured from a financial standpoint, combined with the build-to-order, configure-to-order, and engineer-to-order strategies over time is shown in Figure 3 (AMR Research Report, 2005).

Integrating knowledge-management systems and processes into the workflows of product configuration continue to show significant potential for delivering profitable growth. However, there are several key success factors necessary for this to occur. First, there must be a focus on how to best manage the measurement of performance, and this analysis has concentrated on the hierarchy of supply-chain metrics for this task. Second, there needs to be a focus on how to streamline the quoting and product-configuration processes while measuring the impact of tacit and explicit knowledge, which has been shown for a global manufacturer of electric engines. This approach to defining a taxonomy of knowledge that can scale globally over web-based applications is critical for a business to scale for the long term. Finally, the effect of knowledge integration within product-configuration strategies is measurable from the context of process areas, as is shown in Figure 5 (AMR Research Report, 2005).

This chapter provided an in-depth review of literature related to knowledge management, and its integration with different processes with different metrics. Chapter 2 studied, in depth, the approaches taken by manufacturing companies to capturing knowledge and also to evaluating business processes. Chapter 3 details the methodology adopted by this study to understand how knowledge management is being used today to streamline and make more efficient the service strategies of manufacturing and services companies.

Chapter 3: Research Methodology

The impact of knowledge-management strategies on the build-to-order process delivers significant operational and financially-based gains over time. Being able to design a specific build-to-order process so that it can deliver the maximum results possible is predicated on understanding several critical factors in a business adopting this approach to unifying selling and production. To attain the highest perfect order accuracy, companies adopting the build-to-order process as a selling and service process must first concentrate on the role-based use of knowledge management throughout their enterprises.

Role-based use of knowledge alleviates the potential for errors in order processing and reduces the churn of incorrect orders that must be corrected by a median of seven or more times, and increases the accuracy of long-term product planning and new product launching (Columbus, 2008). The Perfect Order metric captures the extent to which role-based knowledge is being shared throughout an organization. The greater the agility, accuracy, and speed with which a company is using role-based knowledge, the greater the Perfect Order accuracy, operations, and financially-based performance it attains.

The intention of this methodology is to factor the use of role-based knowledge in the build-to-order process, and thereby determine how enterprise, legacy, and previous isolated systems are optimized for performance. Dashboard and the hierarchy of supply-chain metrics are excellent metrics for measuring the broader trends impacting a company over time to be implemented with an internal framework which can quantify performance gains over time. Therefore, this methodology also concentrates on creating this framework of measurable performance gains that are directly attributable to a more accurate and efficient build-to-order process over the long term. Chapter 3 offers a brief description of the adopted research methodology activities, such as research design, research question and sampling strategy, research instrument, data collection procedures, and data analyses.

Research Question

How is knowledge management being used today to streamline and make more efficient the service strategies of manufacturing and services companies?

Purpose of Research

The following are the research objectives of this study:

i.   To evaluate the contributory effects of knowledge management on the mass customization and build-to-order strategies of manufacturing companies in the high-technology industry by measuring Perfect Order accuracy.

ii.   To determine the causality in knowledge-management system integration in build-to-order and mass-customization system performance when varying integration technologies are used, ranging from Electronic Data Interchange (EDI) to RosettaNet and real-time XML integration.

iii. To define a series of dashboard metrics that can be used for evaluating the knowledge-management system contribution to custom configuration and quoting accuracy across all channels through which a manufacturer sells.

iv.   By using the hierarchy of supply chain metrics (Hofman, 2004), to define a maturity model for the integration of knowledge-management systems to product-configuration platforms that enable the build-to-order and mass-customization process.

v.   To devise a framework for quantifying the performance gains of integrating knowledge-management systems and product-configuration strategies.

Each of these objectives will also consider the contributions of role-based knowledge-management strategies for build-to-order selling and fulfillment. As previous studies indicate the greater the role-based delivery of knowledge, the greater the operational and financial performance, this methodology looks to accelerate knowledge and insight in this area (Hofman, 2004; Columbus, 2008). The contribution of role-based knowledge management to the financial impact of build-to-order strategies provides another foundational level of support for each of the research objectives defined in this study. It is the intention of this study to evaluate how role-based knowledge management for the build-to-order strategies of respondents delivers greater levels of financial performance. This study also evaluates the effectiveness of the distinction between using knowledge as a central repository or Master Data Management (MDM) architecture versus its selective use in role-based implementations.

Research Design

The research design includes detailed plans on what, where, and how data are to be collated (Creswell, 2009). In creating this research design, several key assumptions have been made about the use of knowledge-management strategies within the build-to-order process.

At first, knowledge management must be role-based to be as effective as possible in automating the build-to-order process. As previous research has shown, the greater the role-based use of knowledge management, the greater the accuracy, efficiency, and transaction velocity achieved (Hofman, 2004; Columbus, 2008).

The second assumption is that the contributory effects of knowledge management are not linear, but follow an experience curve effect, gradually increasing over time as enterprises gain greater insights into how to align resources to needs. This assumption that growth is not linear is also fundamental to evaluating the impact of role-based knowledge being applied to the build-to-order process. It can be reasonably assumed that the elasticity of knowledge is greater the more rapidly an organization attempts to launch new products and gain market share. This is correlated to the experience effect and points to the need to understand the elasticity of knowledge by role to understand how the build-to-order process can be optimized over time.

The third assumption is that the legacy, internally-developed, and enterprise-wide ERP systems have a significant effect on the overall performance of the build-to-order process. For this study, the ERP systems in use by respondent organizations will be considered and analyzed as part of the results. ERP system integration is also one of the most potentially costly and challenging tasks, for enterprise-system development in support of strategies. This study will encompass the role of ERP systems as a catalyst of greater build-to-order process accuracy, performance, precision, and resulting profitability. ERP system designers have also become more attuned to the need for the role-based use of analytics and knowledge management, creating workflows that also align with the needs of the build-to-order process. Further, ERP vendors will often provide a series of references to their systems in the hope of winning new customers. Capitalizing on these references, this research study looks to gain insights into how these systems contribute to a more effective build-to-order process.

Population and Sample Strategy

The sampling frame for this research is defined as those high-technology manufacturers who rely on build-to-order, configure-to-order, and engineer-to-order workflows as part of their main selling strategies. The respondents will be CFOs and the heads of accounting and finance, as these members of a management team will have insights into the performance of build-to-order, configure-to-order, and engineer-to-order strategies from a profitability standpoint, and have data available for calculating the Perfect Order metric for their companies.

During the literature review process, it was determined that the majority of Chief Information officers (CIOs) report to the CFO of the organizations of which they are members. As a result, the CFO is the primary respondent for this study. The factors supporting this decision to have the CFO as primary respondent rather than the CIO are as follows. First, the CFO has a clearer view of the results being attained by all complex business strategies and processes. A CFO's responsibility is to evaluate the performance of IT investments in terms of their ROI as well. This vantage point, and the access to strategic data on the performance of all strategies, specifically those which are complex and in need of orchestration as build-to-order, also make the CFO the ideal candidate to be the primary respondent for this study. Secondly, the CFO will be more attuned to early adopter results and the evolving set of best practices in the role-based use of knowledge management, and the nascent area of role-based business intelligence which, as was discovered during the literature review, is a critical element in build-to-order strategy success. Thirdly, CFOs are often called on by CEOs to enable the build-to-order process across the entire enterprise. This also includes working with the Chief Marketing officers (CMOs) to complete the entire strategy from the channel and selling side, through manufacturing, to fulfillment. From the literature review, when the CEO appoints the CFO to work with marketing and sales to track the performance of the build-to-order strategies being completed, there is higher accountability and performance over time. As a result of all these factors, the CFO is the primary respondent for this study.

Research Instrument

The survey questionnaire was designed by using Zoomerang, a web-based online survey application. The web-based survey is designed with graphics, and includes a series of trade-offs on choosing to invest in role-based knowledge-management integration to product-configuration systems (used for the build-to-order component), and the use of supply-chain metrics of performance at present and in the future. The surveys ask the respondents to make decisions as to how to use scarce resources for a new product introduction, or how critical knowledge-management systems are for making pricing adjustments mid-point in a product's lifecycle. The POI index will also be covered as part of the questionnaire content, to see if the respondent companies are correlating Perfect Order performance to customer satisfaction. Adoption of role-based knowledge-management systems to support build-to-order strategies will also be included in the questionnaire. The lag-time from implementing build-to-order strategies and the systems supporting it to attaining financial and operations-based metrics will be measured and used as a variable in the analysis.

Data Collection Procedures

The survey was sent to participants via e-mail; participants were contacted through the AEA, and user-groups from Infor, Oracle, SAP, and QAD. This approach ensured the optimal information was gathered. Initial presentations were made to the leaders of the AEA, Infor, Oracle, SAP, and QAD user groups to ensure a high response rate. Confidentiality of responses was assured to ensure a higher response rate. All responses were analyzed entirely anonymously to further protect the confidentiality of the respondents. The leaders of the AEA and user-groups of the Infor, Oracle, SAP, and QAD were informed of the purpose of the study.

Zoomerang has applications for completing data analysis. Data coded in the interval, and ratio-level of analysis, were fed into SPSS Version 19 for further analysis and presentation. The data captured through Zoomerang were verified by checking each IP address that logged into the survey site, to ensure that there was only one login per respondent. In addition, the results were verified by secondary research from leading industry analyst firms to validate the results from a published third party. Verification of results was also attained by mitigating the risk of surveyor bias, by stating the study was purely for academic research and all results would be kept strictly confidential. Assuring confidentiality, the fact the research would be aggregated for academic use, and the request for assistance with academic studies were motivators to persuade companies and user-groups to respond.

Facilitating the research study to ensure a high degree of data reliability and validity are the most critical aspects of any researcher's role. The need to manage the research process to minimize and eliminate researcher bias is critical. The methodology was specifically designed to allow for eliminating interviewer bias by stating the academic intent of the research, and the value which the data collected and analyzed would have for academic research.

Ethical Considerations

Every effort has been made to ensure the highest ethics were attained in completing this study. The rights of the participants were protected by keeping the data profile and response data confidential. Information provided by the respondents will not be shared (American Psychological Association, 2011). The participants were informed of the purpose of the study through email, and their consent was sought, as mentioned above, by providing the details of the nature and purpose of the research, the potential subjects who would have access to the data, and the proposed outcome of the research.

The first ethical concern dealt with the voluntary participation of respondents. The need to have a higher response rate could often lead to conflicts arising from voluntary participation. The second ethical guideline entailed protecting respondents' identities. The researcher protected all information submitted, including the personal details of the respondents. All responses were kept

45

confidential and anonymous, which was intimated to the AEA, Infor, Oracle, SAP, and QAD user-groups as an assurance to gain their cooperation in the survey.

Data Analyses

The process of analyzing data is critical, as it seeks to address the research question, and the researcher emphasized this section to ensure the obtained data were appropriately analyzed to reach valid and reliable conclusions. The collated data were gradually recorded, organized, and analyzed.

The coded data were first downloaded from the web-survey server with a secure connection and into a secured personal computer. To organize, store, and carry out statistical analysis, the researcher used Microsoft Excel, and SPSS® software. The anti-virus and Symantec end-protection software helped prevent hacking and other virus attacks, and kept data secure. After analysis, the data were stored in an offline secured server. Specifically, no paper was used for the completion of this study. The entire study was completed online and through the use of office automation applications included in the Microsoft Office Suite. The results of the statistical analysis are password-protected as SPSS files, stored on a Microsoft Windows-based system that is secured behind a firewall. Back-up data is stored on a USB drive locked in the researcher's desk and secured by a keyed lock.

Summary

This chapter on research methodology offered some valuable insights on how data were collated for the study. Chapter 4 presents the data analysis and results, after studying the collated data.

Chapter 4: Analysis and Presentation of Results

This research aims to understand the application of knowledge management to optimize the build-to-order process in manufacturing and service companies. Chapters 1, 2, and 3 presented the research questions and developed the theoretical foundation through a literature review, and the methodology of the research. Chapter 4 will present the data collected via the self-administered web-based survey instrument.

The reliance on build-to-order processes and strategies continues to accelerate with the catalysts of greater emphasis on customer management, reliance on Software-as-a-Service (SaaS) for unifying diverse selling teams, and the need for gaining higher utilization rates of existing production facilities. The build-to-order process emerges from this analysis as a critical catalyst for ensuring the value chains of businesses become more efficient by embracing lean manufacturing concepts and techniques.

Research Question

How is knowledge management being used today to streamline and make more efficient service strategies of manufacturing and services companies?

Survey Sample and Data Collection Process

A total of 82 participants from manufacturing and service companies in the U.S. successfully completed the survey online, having been contacted through the AEA and user-groups from Infor, Oracle, SAP, and QAD. The results of the survey indicate the pace of build-to-order adoption is increasing. Driven by renewed focus on top-line revenue growth over cost reduction, company CFOs surveyed indicated that a renewed focus on greater lifetime customer value had replaced their efforts to aggressively trim costs. The CFOs had seen the sales pipelines continually improve over the last ten months to a year. This led them to begin investing again in customer-facing initiatives, including build-to-order process strategies. Many CFOs (53%) cited initial efforts to integrate knowledge management into the build-to-order process had been only partially effective. The approach to the role-based use of knowledge management in build-to-order processes has been gaining momentum, according to the CFOs surveyed. What was unexpected in these results was the rapid adoption of role-based knowledge management to support the build-to-order process and all customer-facing strategies.

Based on the survey results, 39.8% had already implemented role-based knowledge management into their build-to-order processes and strategies. Of all approaches to implementing quote-to-order processes and strategies, the majority of respondents were either piloting or rolling out this strategy enterprise-wide on a mainstream product (59%). Further, most of these were implemented using real-time analytics, which is the most costly to integrate, support, and enable over time. The combinations of these findings suggest most of the respondents in the study are second or third generation quote-to-order adopters and have a predetermined roadmap of exactly what they need to accomplish. Survey data indicate the median attempts to streamline the quote-to-order process and integrate knowledge management into the workflows is 3.2 times; this means many companies are going through an adoption and learning curve for integrating knowledge into this process. It is evident there is significant churn in the first two to three generations of companies adopting the quote-to-order process, based on this analysis. Key factors that are leading to churn and driving the quote-to-order replacements are defined in this chapter. Another factor that emerged from the analysis is how critical the ERP system is, as nearly every respondent company relies on this system for analytics reporting, analytics, and developing build-to-order process scorecards. 54.8% of respondents mentioned that getting more value from their build-to-order process was a primary factor in replacing or augmenting their existing ERP system. This validates the assumption that CFOs see the financial and operational performance gains from build-to-order as strategic enough to warrant investment in new enterprise systems.

As the literature review showed that ERP systems are a contributing factor to the success of role-based knowledge-management systems, demographics of respondents in this area were captured. The most common ERP vendor in the respondent base is Oracle, with just over 47% of all companies running their operations on this ERP system. Second is Infor, with 20.7%, followed by SAP, with just over 18%. Table 1, Installed ERP System Used to Support the Quote-to-Order process, shows the distribution of responses by ERP system type.

Table 1

Installed ERP System Used to Support the Quote-to-Order Process

ERP System	Frequency	Percent	Valid Percent	Cumulative Percent
QAD	5	6.1	6.1	5.7
Infor	17	20.7	20.7	27.6
SAP	15	18.3	18.3	46.0
Oracle	39	47.6	47.6	99.2
Internally developed	6	7.3	7.3	100.0
Total	82	100.0	100.0	

Next, the respondents were asked which process areas received the highest priority for investment in terms of integrating ERP, analytics, and knowledge-management systems together, as shown in Table 2. 54.8% of the respondents mentioned the build-to-order process. Tables 3 and 4 provide additional details on how analytics are being used in these companies.

Table 2

Prioritization of Process Areas for ERP, Analytics, and Knowledge-Management Integration Investment

Process Area	Frequency	Percent	Valid Percent	Cumulative Percent
Lean Manufacturing using Kanban	4	4.9	4.9	4.9
Inventory Management	31	37.8	37.8	42.7
Build-to-Order	45	54.8	54.8	97.5
Project-based Manufacturing	2	2.5	2.5	100.0
Total	82	100.0	100.0	

Table 3

ERP-based Analytics and Knowledge Management in Use

Areas	Frequency	Percent	Valid Percent	Cumulative Percent
Department-wide	18	21.9	21.9	21.9
Division-wide	12	14.6	14.6	36.6
Division and channel	13	15.9	15.9	52.4
Corporate-wide	35	42.7	42.7	95.1
Extended supply chain and global manufacturing	4	4.9	4.9	100.0
Total	82	100.0	100.0	

Table 4
What Type of Analytics in Use?

		Frequency	Percent	Valid Percent	Cumulative Percent
Valid	Batch	41	50.0	51.4	51.4
	Real-time	39	47.6	48.6	100.0
	Total	80	97.6	100.0	
Missing	System	2	2.4		
Total		82	100.0		

The implementation strategy of role-based knowledge management to support the quote-to-order process is shown in Table 5. The most dominant strategy is to concentrate on piloting a mainstream product (39.8%) by first integrating role-based knowledge management into the quote-to-order process. This is followed by piloting the integration of role-based knowledge management systems to support build-to-order across the production center (31%).

Table 5

Implementation Strategy for Role-based Knowledge Management to support the Quote-to-Order

Process

	Frequency	Percent	Valid Percent	Cumulative Percent
Pilot on low-volume, low-margin products to minimize risk	9	11.0	14.8	14.8
Pilot in mainstream product line	25	30.5	39.8	54.6
Pilot across entire production center	19	23.2	31.1	85.7
Launch in secondary manufacturing centers and go live	8	9.8	12.8	98.5
Launched with new ERP system implementation				
Total	1	1.2	1.5	100.0
System	62	75.7	100.0	
	20	24.3		
Total	82	100.0		

Analysis of Role-based ERP System Contributions

The demographics indicate that integration of role-based knowledge-management into the workflow of a company is occurring with increasing frequency. The bundling of analytics, BI, and knowledge-management modules into existing ERP systems is drastically reducing the barriers to adopting this strategy. In addition, the stability of ERP systems as the system of record for quote-to-order systems is also reducing the risk associated with accentuating this selling strategy in integrating role-based knowledge management. Table 6, Using ERP-based Analytics Applications for Knowledge Management, Use Case Analysis illustrates how and where respondents are choosing to implement analytics and knowledge management by strategy areas within their companies. When analytics and knowledge management are deployed department-wide, it is most often done to streamline Inventory Management and supply chain areas which concern CFOs. When analytics and role-based knowledge management are deployed across entire corporations, 60% of the time it is done to streamline the quote-to-order process. This supports the finding of quote-to-order having a multigenerational aspect as a business process. The median company contacted during the survey had attempted to implement quote-to-order processes and strategies three times. By the third time, the decision to go corporate-wide had been taken, based on the accumulated experience over previous two implementations. Overcoming resistance to change is the most common initial problem with integrating role-based knowledge management into the build-to-order process. Most respondents mention this as the primary factor in the initial churn of the attempt to infuse intelligence into selling.

Table 6

ERP-based Analytics Applications for Knowledge-Management Use Case Analysis

		ERP-based Analytics in Use					Total
		Department-wide	Division-wide	Division and channel	Corporate-wide	Extended supply chain and global mfg	
Lean Manufacturing	Count	3	0	0	1	0	4
using Kanban	% within ERP-based Analytics in use	17.9%	0.0%	0.0%	2.9%	0.0%	4.9%
Inventory Management	Count	**14**	5	9	9	1	38
	% within ERP-based Analytics in use	**78.6%**	41.7%	69.2%	25.7%	25.0%	46.3%
Quote-to-Order	Count	1	6	4	**21**	2	34
	% within ERP-based Analytics in use	5.5%	50.0%	32.5%	**60.0%**	50.0%	41.5%
Project-based	Count	0	1	0	4	1	6
Manufacturing	% within ERP-based Analytics in use	0.0%	8.3%	0.0%	11.4%	25.0%	7.3%
Total	Count	18	12	13	35	4	82
	% within ERP-based Analytics in use	100.0%	100.0%	100.0%	100.0%	100.0%	

Selection of Metrics

When respondents were asked which specific metrics they relied on to create their scorecards and dashboards, the metrics included in the hierarchy of supply-chain metrics shown in Figure 2 (Hofman, 2004) were specifically listed on the questionnaire. Multiple responses to this question were allowed, as the intention of the research is to capture each metric associated with the process of measuring role-based knowledge management's contribution to the quote-to-order process.

The results indicate the majority of CFOs are operationally focused, with the order-cycle time being the most commonly-used metric to evaluate the effectiveness of analytics and knowledge-management integration. Second, the accuracy of Work in Process (WIP) and Finished Goods (FG) inventory positions was also cited by respondents. Reduction in order re-work, as measured by a reduced Days Sales Outstanding (DSO) level, was considered by CFOs to be the

54

single most effective metric for showing the financial gain of integrating knowledge management into the quote-to-order process. This was because reducing the DSO levels had a direct effect on gaining higher efficiency and greater velocity of cash-to-cash transactions. Only 3% of respondents had calculated the cost to rework or modify an order, and of these, less than 1% was tracking Perfect Order performance. The results of the study show the value of integrating role-based knowledge into a quote-to-order workflow does have an immediate impact on the DSO levels because of order reduction errors and has significant effects on quickening the cash-to-cash conversion cycles. However, it does not necessarily lead to a higher Perfect Order score, as most companies consider demand-forecast accuracy and quote-to-cash cycle times as critical. Adopting the Perfect Order metric was in the most time-sensitive business of all, which is the production of customized integrated circuits. The Perfect Order metric is most valued in the highest-velocity and most time-sensitive business models, including the design and manufacturing of customized integrated circuits. The use of the Perfect Order metric by a semiconductor manufacturer in the sample base supports this finding. The following chapter presents an analysis of results and a framework for integrating role-based knowledge management into the build-to-order workflow.

Details of Analysis and Results

The transition of manufacturing companies from cost reduction to top-line revenue growth as a means to attain profitability is in full force, according to the results of this analysis. With build-to-order processes being the single most important factor in revamping, augmenting, or replacing ERP systems, there continues to be a corresponding growth in the purchasing of knowledge-management applications to support this strategy. 42.7% of respondents have corporate-wide ERP systems in place that include role-based knowledge management that also can deliver real-time financial metrics of performance. 54.8% are primarily focusing on the quote-to-order process, using ERP-based analytics to streamline and automate this business process. 37.8% of respondents are migrating to the quote-to-order process to attain supply chain optimization objectives, looking to streamline their inventory management and lean manufacturing Kanban strategies (4.9%).

Resistance to change, the single greatest factor that forces enterprise initiatives to fail, is also present in the quote-to-order processes that CMOs and CFOs are attempting to implement. When asked which factor most contributed to longer pilot times, CFOs were unanimous in resistance to change, and a lack of system adoption, as being the leading causes of a quote-to-order process failing. With the typical company taking an average of up to three iterations of their quote-to-order process to get the workflows, reporting and integration to selling, and production and logistics systems functioning to a level that makes the strategy financially viable, CFOs most often pointed to a lack of change management as the leading factor in forcing churn. There is much empirically-derived evidence that change management is the single greatest cause of enterprise system failure, and the failure of technology investments to attain the financial results expected (Alstyne, Brynjolfsson, Madnick, 1995).

From the survey, it was discovered that many sales managers, sales reps, manufacturing managers, and production scheduling managers perceived the intensive use of role-based knowledge management as a means to capture their expertise and minimize their roles in the organization. The fear that their jobs would eventually be more tightly controlled, using the analytics, and that, ultimately, their pay would be reduced, led to many of the sales team initially refusing to work with the front-end quoting, sales, and product configuration systems. Earlier, the statistic was mentioned that, on average, it takes an enterprise about three iterations to get their build-to-order process implemented well enough to attain the financial and operations-based

56

results they initially expected. From the research completed, it can be reasonably assumed that aligning role-based knowledge-management systems to sales, marketing, manufacturing, and logistics takes, on average, at least one iteration of a quote-to-order process design.

This finding is supported by a series of results gained through the surveys. This factor is also what led to one-third of respondents choosing to complete pilots of role-based knowledge-management integration in their quote-to-order systems. Integrating role-based knowledge management into the quote-to-order process was enabled by the ERP platforms on which companies had been standardized. CFOs, when surveyed about this aspect of adopting role-based knowledge management in their build-to-order processes and strategies, mentioned that bundling analytics and business intelligence (BI) at no cost by ERP vendors served as one of the key catalysts in enabling the pilots to be completed. ERP vendors have typically bundled in analytics and BI tools and applications as part of ERP upgrades, and to substantiate the relatively high maintenance prices they charge, which can be up to 22% of the purchase price of an ERP system. The CFOs explained that having the analytics, BI and knowledge-management modules bundled into the price of their ERP systems made it more affordable to finance pilots and eventual integration into the build-to-order processes. The maintenance pricing of 22% or more had made integrating role-based knowledge management into the quote-to-order process more cost-effective and driven up the ROI of pilots quickly. This explains why many respondents moved directly into a full launch enterprise-wide on a main product line. The software applications had already been purchased through maintenance contracts, even though the ERP vendors selling to these companies had bundled them into the systems already installed. As a result, this tactic by ERP vendors created a catalyst for role-based knowledge management and role-based business intelligence in quote-to-order process companies. Only 40% of respondents were focused on risk-averse approaches to testing the integration of role-based knowledge management in their quote-to-order processes, which is consistent with previous comparable studies of ERP adoption (MacCrimmon & Wehrung, 1990). Mitigating risk through pilots, however, has been shown to be the most effective strategy there is for evaluating enterprise-wide sell-side strategies before going live enterprise-wide (Luo & Strong, 2004).

Summary of Results

The research results indicate that CFOs are integrating role-based knowledge management into their quote-to-order processes, yet only after completing a median three tries before getting it right. The first iteration is most often attributed to change-management initiatives, with second and third iterations being attributed to the role-based analysis of sales, manufacturing, and logistics' managers' information needs. Most implementations are done on a department-wide basis first, with risk being mitigated through pilots when role-based knowledge management is used for solving the supply-chain aspects of quote-to-order first. The next chapter, on analysis and recommendations, provides a framework for evaluating the long-term financial impact of integrating knowledge management into the build-to-order process and analyzes the results from the context of the research objectives.

Chapter 5: Conclusions and Recommendations

The overall research question addressed by this study was: How is knowledge management being used today to streamline and make more efficient service strategies of manufacturing and services companies? Equating the investments in quote-to-order and build-to-order selling and knowledge-management initiatives to financial performance is a critical link that many senior managers and CFOs report as the highest priority for their firms going forward (54.8%). While complex selling and knowledge-management initiatives are made in pilot-based approaches in most instances, respondents to the survey report that corporate-wide adoption of quote-to-order and build-to-order initiatives are becoming commonplace (47.5%). Therefore, companies adopt a pilot-based approach to defining their enterprise computing strategies. The greatest is to reduce the risk of failure because of a lack of change management planning and execution (Luo & Strong, 2004). Aligning the quote-to-order and build-to-order strategies at the process level to the specific needs and requirements of each department is a critical success factor in any implementation. The results of this research continue to support this finding from the broader body of research completed.

In completing this analysis, the factors of corporate- or enterprise-wide deployment of quote-to-order strategies, with effective change-management strategies, have the potential to yield significant financial gains over time. To attain this analysis from the study, the series of supply-chain metrics most often used form the foundation of this data analysis. The research shows most CFOs are primarily focused on order-cycle time (75%) followed by WIP and FG inventory levels (62%). Throughout the study, the issues surrounding DSO continued to be a priority to respondents, as the majority sees this metric as a measure of inventory velocity and overall efficiency. DSOs are also essential for evaluating the cash-to-cash conversion cycle inherent in quote-to-order and build-to-order strategies that are efficient and profitable.

This chapter concentrates on the causality of the research results to the broader financial performance of the firms surveyed, over the long term. It addresses those research objectives of the study which include how to streamline complex selling and service strategies in manufacturing and services using knowledge management and define which metrics companies are using to manage and evaluate their knowledge-management systems. How these metrics and KPIs contribute to the Perfect Order process is specifically analyzed in this chapter, including a series of analyses about how the distributed order-management process can be made more efficient by using the insights gained. Finally, it addresses an analysis to support the research objective of how effective knowledge-management systems are in alleviating churn and increasing customer satisfaction.

Discussion of the Results

Assessing the Build-to-Order and Quote-to-Order's Impact on Streamlining Complex Selling and Service Strategies

The decision by respondents to concentrate on quote-to-order and build-to-order strategies most of the time as a means to monetize their investments in knowledge management (54.8%), followed by inventory management (37.8%), and lean manufacturing (4.9%), shows that the transition is now occurring from cost reductions driven by economies of scale, to those driven by intelligent manufacturing (Dagdeviren, 2010).

Supporting this move to more intelligent manufacturing is the decision by respondents to concentrate on real-time analysis in a large percentage of implementations (48.6%), with inventory management measured on a department-wide basis (78.6%). Further evidence of how pervasive the shift is from cost-based to intelligent manufacturing can be found in an analysis of the integration strategies that respondents are relying on to create more efficient complex selling and service strategies. 19% of respondents are integrating ERP, pricing, and CRM systems together, while approximately 30% are using shell scripting and advanced PERL-based programming to integrate systems at the process and application level. 9% are attaining best practices in integration by using SOAs that provide a platform foundation of analytics and measurement. The respondents have had the greatest success in streamlining and making more efficient the complex selling and service strategies of manufacturing and services organizations in their companies. The wide adoption rate of analytics, based on this sample, also supports the finding of how respondents are moving more towards knowledge-sharing networks. Developing knowledge-driven networks predicated on quote-to-order, build-to-order, and knowledge-management integration is one of the key catalysts of companies attaining higher levels of financial performance as a result.

The results show that developing knowledge-sharing networks is accelerated by the continual tacit and implicit knowledge shared during creating and fine-tuning the quote-to-order and build-order processes. The trajectory of growth within the organizations that seek to streamline their complex build-to-order and quote-to-order processes parallels those found in heavy equipment and automotive manufacturing companies as well. A case in point is the continual evolution of the knowledge-sharing networks of Toyota Production System. The maturation process of knowledge-sharing networks that occurred within Toyota over a decade of study is shown in Figure 6 (Dyer & Nobeoka, 2000).

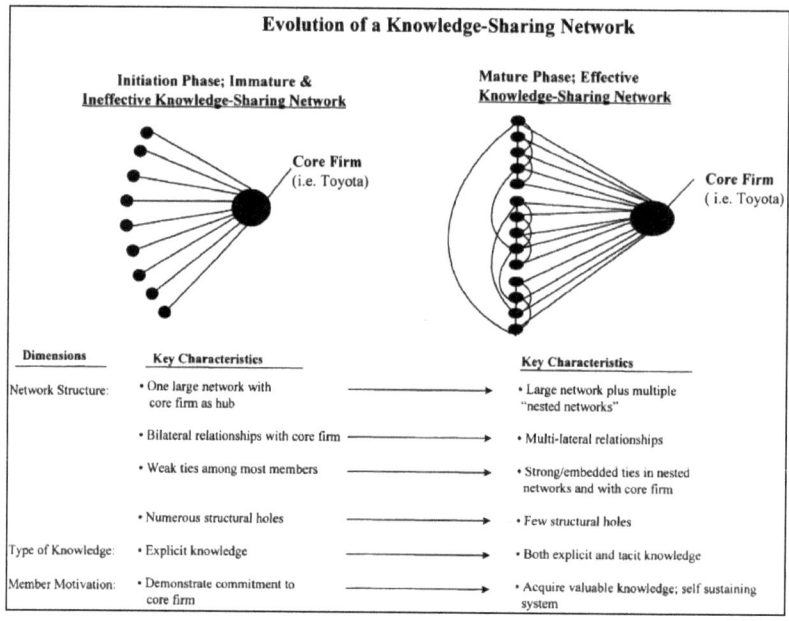

Figure 6. Evolution of the Toyota Knowledge-Sharing Network.

Knowledge management is used as an accelerator for moving from cost reduction IT strategies to relying on knowledge as a means to create greater financial value. This study found that respondent organizations are at various stages of maturity, moving from cost-reduction strategies to reliance on knowledge as the basis of competitive strength. A maturity model emerges from the analysis, showing how the level and pervasiveness of knowledge use throughout the build-to-order and quote-to-order strategies impacts financial performance over time. A causal relationship emerges from how a company manages its knowledge in the build-to-order and quote-to-order strategy, based on these findings; as a result, they align well to a multi-stage maturity model. Figure 7 shows a depiction of a proposed knowledge-sharing maturity model that emerges from the analysis.

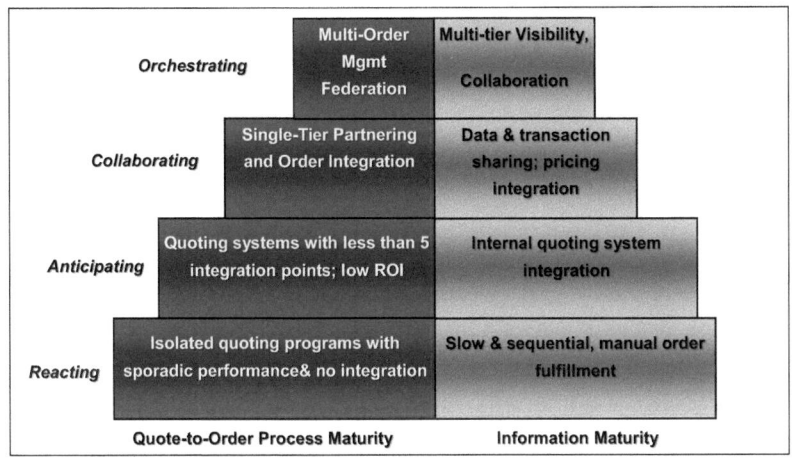

	Quote-to-Order Process Maturity	Information Maturity
Orchestrating	Multi-Order Mgmt Federation	Multi-tier Visibility, Collaboration
Collaborating	Single-Tier Partnering and Order Integration	Data & transaction sharing; pricing integration
Anticipating	Quoting systems with less than 5 integration points; low ROI	Internal quoting system integration
Reacting	Isolated quoting programs with sporadic performance& no integration	Slow & sequential, manual order fulfillment

Figure 7. Proposed Knowledge-Sharing Maturity Model.

The greater the quote-to-order process maturity throughout a company, the greater the information maturity and velocity of data shared across suppliers and channel partners, and throughout the quote-to-order and build-to-order strategies and processes. The proposed knowledge-sharing maturity model shows how the stratification of respondents by group, based on their information maturity influences and significantly drives the level of quote-to-order process maturity as a result.

This finding, based on the analysis of the research data, shows that the greater the level of separation or isolation of a given quoting or pricing strategy, the less likely the organization will be to be able to recover and grow their quote-to-order and build-to-order process profitability, even with best practices in knowledge management being present. Those companies in the lowest sections of the maturity model were mostly completing pilots of build-to-order and configure-to-order strategies. They were also relying on manually-based approaches to defining their overall proposal generation, pricing, quoting, and Bill of Materials (BOM) integration. As a result of this heavy reliance on manually-based approaches to completing quoting, proposal generation, pricing, and BOM integration, companies on this stratum of the maturity model are often reacting, rather than planning how they will manage customer demand. This, in turn, results in relatively high levels of DSO performance, with order-rework rates being increased. When a given order needs to be re-worked on average seven times through a custom truck manufacturing process, it is a sign that the knowledge integration with the selling process is either not reliable, or non-existent. As a result of the time constraints of this study, it was not possible to individually evaluate and analyze each company in the survey. Given how manually based the quote-to-order and build-to-order processes are on the reacting level of this maturity model, it is clear there is much room for improvement.

Analyzing just which aspects of the build-to-order and configure-to-order processes and strategies need to improve first was possible, given the data sets. Companies occupying this stratum are mainly measuring only gross sales, quoting accuracy at a very isolated, per-product level, and only evaluating integration at the accounting system, rather than the quoting, pricing, or ERP level as they relate to Perfect Order. Therefore, companies occupying this the maturity model are slow in reacting to market conditions, slow in solving complex quoting problems, and challenged in making complex engineer-to-order products profitable. The potential exists with build-to-order, configure-to-order, and engineer-to-order strategies to gain far higher levels of margins than are possible on standard make-to-stock products. However, to attain these margins, there needs to be a minimal integration across departments and, most critically, for the sell-side strategies of a business (including proposals, quoting, and pricing) to be linked with the back-office systems including ERP, logistics, and fulfillment. Without those system integration points, and where there is a lack of analytics to track the performance of the build-to-order and quote-to-order strategies throughout the company, many companies on the reacting stratum or layer of the maturity model will eventually exit the build-to-order and configure-to-order strategies, because of the lack of profits they generate. From a cursory analysis, it appears to be a lack of planning and synchronization which leads to companies exiting these strategies. In fact, it is the lack of coordination and support for knowledge-management workflows, and the ability to transform their tacit and implicit knowledge into a sustainable competitive advantage over time.

The respondents that occupy the reacting layer of the model are often driven to compete only on price, which leads to commoditization of markets and a drastic reduction in profitability. From analyzing the results of companies on this layer of the model, it is apparent that a lack of well-defined and well-executed strategies for knowledge management leads companies to compete on price first and foremost, often forsaking their innate competitive strengths. In fact, this lowest layer of the maturity model illustrates what happens when the focus shifts only the department, rather than the operating group, or the broader corporate needs for knowledge. The maturity model is predicated on the finding that those respondents who gained the best results invested in information systems, technologies, and processes to set the foundation for a knowledge-sharing network (Dyer & Nobeoka, 2000).

Contrasting the reacting layer of the maturity model of the proposed Knowledge-Sharing Maturity Model with that of the collaborating and orchestrating layers shows how effective knowledge management is a catalyst of profitable, consistent, economic growth. Those companies on the collaborating layer of the model have the ability to track their DSOs, define strategies for reducing them, track inventory costs, and have metrics associated with the entire cash-to-cash cycle for their companies, to the divisional level. This makes it possible for these companies to also track total Supply Chain Management (SCM) costs, while also getting a measure of their

Perfect Order performance. Companies on this stratum of the maturity model are more focused on how to ensure each proposal, quote, and order is accurate and can be fulfilled without impacting other areas of the supply-chain operations or manufacturing scheduling. Respondent companies on the collaborating layer are also seeing the financial benefits of a streamlined knowledge-management process, from the initial analytics to the long-term sharing of product and process knowledge. The respondents on this level of the maturity model see single-tier partnering and order-integration-supporting data and transaction-sharing translating their build-to-order strategies into profitability. This is how the progression of the TPS occurred over time, making the Toyota supply chain and rapid NPDI process more efficient (Dyer & Nobeoka, 2000). Respondent companies on the collaborating layer of the model show that these strategies are more quantified from the standpoints of operations performance, quality control and quality management, and, most importantly, profitability. The greater the information fluidity and agility across departments on the collaboration level of the maturity model, the greater the operations' results and potential for profitable growth. From the respondent base, it is anticipated that one out of every five respondents are on the collaborating layer of the Knowledge-Sharing Maturity Model. This is consistent with studies of comparable maturity models, specifically in supply-chain networks, and developing knowledge-sharing networks across diverse value chains.

The respondents who are the most effective at streamlining and making more efficient their complex selling and service strategies are on the orchestrating layer of the Knowledge-Sharing Maturity Model. The respondents on this level of the model are more focused on how to create multi-channel visibility and collaboration, and also ensure a high level of integration with their distributed-order management systems. Only 5% of all respondents on this level of the Knowledge-Sharing Maturity Model have attained this performance through reliance on SOA and enterprise-wide deployments of IT infrastructures that have analytics across all touch points and systems. Respondents on the orchestrating level of the Knowledge-Sharing Maturity Model also have a high level of operations-based data, and insight into how the overall quoting, proposal management, pricing, ordering, and sell-side systems integrate with ERP, logistics, and supply-chain systems as well. The value chain of their businesses is highly quantified, as evidenced by the high level of investment in real-time system integration and analytics. The 5% of the respondent companies on the orchestrating layer of the model also have made analytics a core area of their IT strategies, and have greater insight into their quote-to-cash and cash-to-cash processes than any other stratum or level of the model. The companies on the orchestrating layer of the model also have stronger demand visibility and more effective demand-forecasting tools than those on any other level.

All these factors contribute to the respondent companies on the orchestrating layer being able to rapidly introduce new products and orchestrate demand forecasts across all of their channels, supply chain partners, and service providers. Respondents operating on the orchestrating layer have attained the level of knowledge-management synchronization that is exemplified in the studies of the TPS and its ability to transform intelligence into cost savings and competitive advantages with each product generation (Dyer & Nobeoka, 2000). Respondent organizations on the orchestrating layer of the Knowledge-Sharing Maturity Model exhibit best practices in knowledge management to streamline their build-to-order and configure-to-order workflows.

Those respondents at the anticipating and collaborating stages of the Knowledge Sharing Maturity Model are in various stages of maturity in implementing their to-order strategies. Nearly all the respondents who are on these two layers of the maturity model have created a high level of integration on the customer-facing sides of their businesses with quoting and proposal systems that report back accurate pricing, Capable-To-Promise and realistic Available-to-Promise dates. As a result, respondents on these layers of the maturity model have the ability to track quote-to-cash and cash-to-cash metrics of performance, and can also determine how their businesses are performing from any inventory management and DSO level.

The respondents on the collaborating level of the model have processes for tracking the level of DSO reductions over time and can infer the level of customer satisfaction over time as well. Respondents on this level also have the ability to track demand forecasts and the impact their build-to-order and configure-to-order strategies over time. They can infer the inflection point of profitability in these strategies, and what they need to achieve corporate-wide profitability as a result. The progression from anticipating to collaborating level of the maturity model is most closely tied to the ability of respondent organizations to be able to quickly translate their implicit and tacit knowledge into financial gain by streamlining their quote-to-order, build-to-order, and product configuration strategies over the long term.

The Knowledge-Sharing Maturity Model is developed to create a framework for defining how knowledge management is being used today to make complex selling and services strategies more efficient. The distribution of the respondents by level of the Knowledge-Sharing Maturity Model used Factor Analysis within SPSS Windows 19 to determine if there were statistically significant differences between groups. The analysis shows there is a significant difference between those respondents who have attained an orchestration level of performance relative to any other, attaining statistical significance at the 0.01 level of confidence. This top tier of respondents, just 5% of the total survey population, benefited from a legacy of SOA, infrastructure investment, and pervasive IT systems integration. The remainder of the respondents was distributed across the layers of the maturity model as follows: 20% on the collaborating layer, 30% on the anticipating

68

layer, and nearly half, 45%, on the reacting layer.

The results indicate most manufacturing companies contacted are at various stages of maturity in streamlining their proposal, quoting, and pricing strategies, yet the majority lack back-office integration. From the customers' standpoint, this translates into an incomplete, and often confusing, experience every time a build-to-order or quote-to-order based product is ordered. It also translates into greater cycles for order-reworked orders, and a higher level of DSOs than those companies on the collaborating layer of the Knowledge-Sharing Maturity Model. Most companies, 75%, are on the anticipating and reacting layers of the model. This equates to literally billions of dollars of revenue a year tied up in system inefficiency, lower customer satisfaction, and, over time, lost customers and market share.

Analysis of Knowledge-Management Metrics relative to The Perfect Order

This study further analyzes the metrics and KPIs relative to the Perfect Order, and how the use of these metrics varies on each layer of the Knowledge-Sharing Maturity Model. The greater the collaboration and synchronization of processes, the more the metrics and KPIs in use by the respondent base are enterprise-wide in scope, not just focused on a given external process or single strategy. This is consistent with several other studies completed by the use of analytics across a broad range of customer-based strategies and initiatives that showed how metrics and KPIs became a political tool to resist large-scale change (Alstyne, Brynjolfsson, Madnick, 1995). Beginning at the reacting layer of the Knowledge-Sharing Maturity Model, the most prevalent metrics related to the Perfect Order are centered on the most fundamental aspects of operational effectiveness. These include the use of order capture rates, average sales price per order, the number of special pricing requests completed, and the number of bad or incomplete orders completed. The costs associated with these metrics are often unknown on the reacting layer of the Knowledge-Sharing

Maturity Model. As the maturity of a company progresses, it attains greater levels of process and system integration, making it possible to understand the costs associated with each of the metrics and KPIs associated with the build-to-order and quote-to-order strategies it is operating. Table 7, showing Quote-to-Order Measures of Performance by Process Area, is a compilation of insights gained from the survey, and also from a series of previous studies pertaining to build-to-order and quote-to-order performance over time (Maull & Weaver, 1995; McAlary, 1999; Mandal & Gunasekaran, 2003).

Table 7

Quote-to-Order Measures of Performance by Process Area

Areas of Measurement	Baseline: What to Measure	Quote-to-Order Performance Evidence
Company-specific	Project costs and expenses	Use as a baseline for defining ROI
	Number of orders per year	Determine configuration's impact on inventory turns
	Current inventory and costs	Inventory turn savings
	Customer Data	Lifetime cost per customer; avg. deal size by customer
Sales	Order cycle time	Order cycle times reduction of 65% or more recorded with mftrs contacted
	Cost of Sales	DSOs reduction from 60 to 29 days on average
	Cross-sell and up-sell revenue	Increase of 33% on aggregate
	Average sales price per order	Increase from 9% to 26%
Quoting and Ordering	Average costs to complete an order	95% reduction in cost per order
	Special Pricing Requests	Over 100% ROI on automating Special Pricing Requests
	Bad or incomplete orders	Incomplete order reductions of 20%

Customer Service	Number of customer complaints	98% reduction in cost of simple requests
	Revenue lost to churn	60% when cross-selling is used with quote-to-order
	Number of calls on order status	Median level of 500 per week to 70
Warranty and Returns	Reduction in warranty cost on customized products	10% reduction at a minimum
	Labor cost reductions	Decrease order re-work from 15% to 2%

Table 7 shows by functional area how companies measure the contributions to operational, manufacturing, and financial performance over time. The key finding from this research is that the greater the level of information maturity that enables quote-to-order process maturity throughout a company, the greater the ability to track financial performance over time. This is especially the case in the areas of current inventory, inventory-carrying costs on supply-chain performance, and the implications of these costs on demand forecasting and the cash-to-cash sales cycle over time. All of these elements taken together contribute to greater insights into how companies align their strategies to the hierarchy of supply-chain metrics.

The focus on streamlining the Perfect Order can also be seen in an analysis of the workflows throughout a typical manufacturer who adopts quote-to-order as a strategy for increasing knowledge use throughout their organization. Attaining Higher Levels of Production Efficiency by Integrating Knowledge Management into Production Workflows, Figure 8, shows the many benefits of integrating knowledge management into the build-to-order and quote-to-order processes of a typical manufacturer.

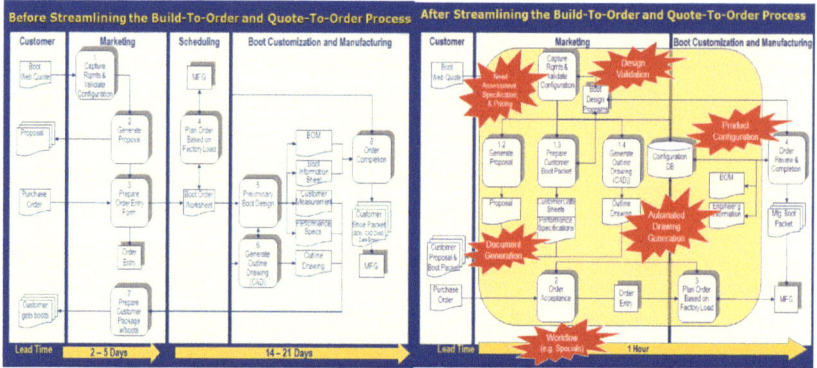

Figure 8. Attaining Higher Levels of Production Efficiency by Integrating Knowledge Management into Production Workflows.

Conclusions and Practical Recommendations

The concepts, framework, and implications of the Knowledge-Sharing Maturity Model on the use of analytics to measure build-to-order and quote-to-order performance show much potential to streamline operations and manufacturing, and increase profitability over time. Each stratum of the Knowledge-Sharing Maturity Model has a different series of metrics associated with it, and the higher up the maturity model a company is, the more likely that its financial systems are tracking the performance of sell-side strategies throughout the manufacturing process. One of the key objectives of the study was to focus on how to alleviate customer churn. By using business-process improvement, as shown in Figure 8, companies can increase customer satisfaction while reducing the DSO levels over time. This yields higher margins as a result of the greater customer-centricity derived from how the processes themselves are designed. The research objectives of the study have been defined and answered using the framework of the Knowledge-Sharing Maturity Model.

The pressure to increase the versatility and customization of production strategies to meet the increasingly eclectic nature of customers' requirements has in its challenges the opportunity for greater profits as well. The continued growth of mass customization as a strategy, however, is raising the expectations of consumers, often leading to their demanding near real-time response to their questions, sales support requests, transactions, and after-purchase customer service. The intention of the research completed has been to show how the build-to-order and configure-to-order processes in manufacturing companies can contribute significant profitability while, at the same time, reducing costs and errors. The critical aspect of these strategies has shown and will continue to show how effective companies are at integrating knowledge management into their product customization workflows over time. This research effort has looked at how best to integrate knowledge management into the build-to-order and configure-to-order workflows of companies.

The findings suggest that a maturity model exists, stratifying companies across a range of information and quote-to-order process areas. The recommendations included in this analysis are defined by each layer of the maturity model, focusing on the practical and pragmatic, as these research results could potentially be used in the future for guiding the development of more thorough implementation of these concepts, and attaining a high level of process and system integration over time. With these concepts and frameworks in mind, the following series of recommendations are made by each stratum or maturity of the proposed Knowledge-Sharing Maturity Model, a framework derived from the research completed.

At this level, the extent of system and process integration is minimal, and often the proposal, quoting, and pricing processes are manual. Only a small percentage of these companies have the ability to electronically track quotes from one-quarter to the next, and many do not have the ability to completely analyze all quotes for a given year. This presents a very significant cost drain on their businesses, as often quotes are produced for products that are actually more expensive to customize than the profits generated from their sale. In other words, product strategies at this level abound with unprofitable products with highly unprofitable configurations. Secondly, there are also quoting systems at this level which are completely disconnected from all other selling systems, often leading to CRM systems having attachments included in records on a very sporadic and incomplete basis. This leads to further confusion, and a lack of consistent disciplines and standards with regard to how quoting is managed. This is also the area of the model, or stratum, where the level of order errors is high, with one respondent mentioning it took on average seven iterations to get the actual order correct. Pricing is also managed from a purely manual standpoint, often only through Microsoft Excel spreadsheets and using manually-based systems over time.

This lowest stratum of the market, which accounts for approximately 45% of total respondents, is marked with a high degree of manual, disconnected, and often highly costly processes. The first recommendation for this stratum of companies is to define which aspect of product configuration makes the most sense for their unique product strategies and requirements, and how pricing can be integrated into the quoting and product-configuration processes in real-time. The product complexity of the product itself also needs to be considered by any company occupying this stratum of the Knowledge-Sharing Maturity Model. The decision to pursue guided selling, sales configuration only or quoting, or product configuration needs to be addressed first from a product-strategy standpoint. This decision point will also define the decision as to which products to include over the long term. Many of these companies selectively choose which systems to integrate based on their level of performance over the long term. Making the quote-to-order and product-configuration strategies as efficient and lean as possible needs to be incorporated into any initial analysis.

This chapter concludes the study, by presenting a summary and discussion of the results in the context of the literature. It is interpreted from the findings that better alignment of processes with customer requirements would help to achieve higher margins in manufacturing and services companies.

References

Alstyne, M., Brynjolfsson, E., & Madnick, S. (1995). Why Not One Big Database? Principles for Data Ownership. *Decision Support Systems, 15,* 267-284.

American Psychological Association. (2011). Retrieved from http://www.apa.org/ethics/code/index.aspx. Accessed on 31st March 2011.

AMR Research Report. (2001). *Building a Case for the Private Trading Exchange.* Boston: Author

AMR Research Report. (2003). *Configuration is the Heart of Customer Fulfillment for Complex Product Manufacturers.* Boston: Author

AMR Research Report. (2005). *The handbook for becoming demand driven.* Boston: Author

Barrett, J. (2007). Demand-Driven is an Operational Strategy. *Industrial Management, 49* (6), 14-19.

Chang, H. H., & Wang, C. I. (2011). Enterprise Information Portals in support of business process, design teams and collaborative commerce performance. *International Journal of Information Management, 31* (2), 171-182.

Choudhary, A., Harding, J., & Tiwari, M. (2009). Data mining in manufacturing: a review based on the kind of knowledge. *Journal of Intelligent Manufacturing, 20* (5), 501-521.

Columbus, L. (2008). The Perfect Order Meets Customer Expectations. *Supply & Demand Chain Executive, 9* (4), 37-38.

Creswell, J.W. (2009). *Research Design. Qualitative, Quantitative and Mixed Methods Approaches.* (3rd ed.). Beverly Hills, CA: Sage.

Dagdeviren, M. (2010). A hybrid multi-criteria decision-making model for personnel selection in manufacturing systems. *Journal of Intelligent Manufacturing, 21* (4), 451-460.

Davison, L., & Al-Shaghana, K. (2007). The Link between Six Sigma and Quality Culture - An Empirical Study. *Total Quality Management & Business Excellence, 18* (3), 249.

Dyer, J. H., & Nobeoka, K. (2000). Creating and managing a high-performance knowledge-sharing network: The Toyota case. *Strategic Management Journal, 21* (3), 345-367.

Fields, G. (2006). Innovation, Time, and Territory: Space and the Business Organization of Dell Computer. *Economic Geography, 82* (2), 119-146.

Foreman, J., Gallien, J., Alspaugh, J., Lopez, F., Bhatnagar, R., Teo, C.C., & Dubois, C. (2010). Implementing Supply-Routing Optimization in a Make-to-Order Manufacturing Network. *Manufacturing & Service Operations Management, 12* (4), 547-568.

Hofman, D. (2004). The Hierarchy of Supply Chain Metrics. *Supply Chain Management Review, 8* (6), 28-37.

Hong, G., Xue, D., & Tu, Y. (2010). Rapid identification of the optimal product configuration and its parameters based on customer-centric product modeling for one-of-a-kind production. *Computers in Industry, 61* (3), 270.

Kenett, R. S. (2009). By Design. *Six Sigma Forum Magazine, 9* (1), 27-29.

Lahl, D. (2011). Make Better Decisions by Analyzing Structured and Unstructured Data Together. *Business Intelligence Journal, 16* (1), 9-16.

Luo, W., & Strong, D. M. (2004). A Framework for Evaluating ERP Implementation Choices. *IEEE Transactions on Engineering Management, 51* (3), 322-333.

MacCrimmon, K. R., & Wehrung, D. A. (1990). Characteristics of Risk Taking Executives. *Management Science, 36* (4), 422-435.

Mandal. P., & Gunasekaran, A. (2003). Issues in implementing ERP: A case study. *European Journal of Operational Research, 146* (2), 274-283.

Maull, R. S., Weaver, A.M., Childe, S.J., Smar, P.A., & Bennett, J. (1995). Current issues in business process re-engineering. *International Journal of Operations & Production Management, 15* (11), 37-52.

McAlary, S. (1999). Three Pitfalls in ERP Implementation. *Strategy & Leadership, 27* (6), 49-50.

Novack, R.A., & Thomas, D. J. (2004). The Challenges of Implementing the Perfect Order Concept. *Transportation Journal, 43* (1), 5-16.

Raisinghani, M., Ette, H., Pierce, R., Cannon, G., & Daripaly, P. (2005). Six Sigma: concepts, tools, and applications. *Industrial Management & Data Systems, 105* (4), 491-505.

Sana, S. S. (2011). A production-inventory model of imperfect quality products in a three-layer supply chain. *Decision Support Systems, 50* (2), 539-547.

Song, Z., & Kusiak, A. (2009). Optimising product configurations with knowledge management and data-mining approach. *International Journal of Production Research, 47* (7), 1733-1751.

Tseng, T., Leeper, T., Banda, C., Herren, S. M., & Ford, J. (2004). Quality Assurance in Machining Process Using Data Mining. *Proceedings from the Industrial Engineering Research.*

Yeh, R., Liu, C., Shia, B., & Huwang, Y. (2008). Imputing manufacturing material in data mining. *Journal of Intelligent Manufacturing, 19* (1), 109-118.

Zhen, L., Jiang, Z., & Song, H. (2011). Distributed knowledge sharing for collaborative product development. *International Journal of Production Research, 49* (10), 2959.